Cover Painting: "Black Grayling" by Joyce Saulsbury

This is an official *Trout Adventures Book* that is part of a series of books about fly fishing the world.

The cover painting is a Khovsgol Black Grayling found only in Khovsgol Nur in Mongolia. The lake is the most pristine lake in the world with water that is potable without treatment. It is also one of the oldest lakes at over two million years old.

ISBN-13: 978-1511510905
ISBN-10: 1511510900

Contents

Dedication

This book is dedicated to my Dad. He had the time to go with me on my first grayling trip and it is the one I have never forgotten.

Acknowledgments

The cover painting "Khovsgol Black Grayling" is by Joyce Saulsbury.
Photo of Baikal Black Grayling and content page grayling are by Brett Hayes.
Photos of Amur Grayling forms are by Mikhail Skopets. His book *Fly Fishing Russia The Far East* provides more detailed information on this part of Russia.
Photos of Yellowtail Grayling are by Clemens Ratschan.
Photos of Upper Lena Grayling are by Alexander Antonov.
Photos of Kamchatka bears are by David Vegnes
I greatly appreciate the help and interest by Igor Knizhin.
All other photos are by the author.

I will forever be indebted to my friend Hishgee who showed me Mongolia.

Introduction

I grew up infatuated with grayling. I discovered them in a fishing magazine when I was a kid and couldn't believe that there was a freshwater fish with a dorsal fin like a sailfish. I caught my first grayling when I was a teenager. I walked into Grebe Lake in Yellowstone National Park with my Dad. We had a great time and caught many grayling that day. That introduction created a passion for grayling that has lasted all of my life. I hadn't planned to do a book on grayling. Then I began catching these wonderful fish that had marvelous colors and had to write about them. **The Complete Book about Grayling** was created out of that passion for the fish and a love of travel. To borrow a phrase from Izaak Walton this book is for the Honest Angler who loves to fish for fun and recreation. It is about finding something new and exploring the world. This book gives a glimpse of the fish and the places where they live.

Grayling live in beautiful places. This is Lake Khovsgol in northern Mongolia.

My grayling adventure became worldwide when I began searching the world for trout. I began writing a series of books about catching all of the world's trout and grayling became part of the story. During my travels I kept an eye out for grayling. There were many trips but there was always time to spend a few days fishing for grayling. Different looking grayling began to turn up. I began catching fish that didn't look like anything in the literature. It became obvious that my grayling studies were incomplete. I had to find out more and do more grayling fishing. I took some grayling trips. These trips allowed me to learn more about grayling and explore the world. Grayling live around the Arctic Circle and share the honor of being one of the most northern fish. There are a few isolated populations that were stranded after the last Ice Age and these isolated fish represent the most southern range of grayling on each continent.

The first grayling I caught were not large and for almost twenty years a thirteen inch fish was the largest I had ever seen. That changed when I began catching fish outside of North America. The largest grayling are in Mongolia and the smallest in North Korea. I did say that Mongolia had the largest grayling when I was in Russia and my comment led to a heated discussion with a Russian guide. That argument lasted for a while and I didn't realize that Russians were that sensitive about grayling. I am now more careful when I mention where the largest grayling live.

There are two basic types of grayling. The Arctic Grayling (*Thymallus arcticus*) can be found around the Arctic Circle until it reaches Europe. Europe has the Proper Grayling (*Thymallus thymallus*) or European Grayling in most northern areas on the Continent and British Isles. I don't normally use scientific names in my books but it is the only way to keep grayling straight. I hope those that enjoy fishing for grayling will be patient as the scientific names show up in the book. The two basic types are well established and widely distributed. All grayling subspecies are some form of Arctic Grayling. I have found fourteen different Arctic Grayling subspecies and many of them live side-by-side. Scientific specialists that classify grayling call this sympatry. Sympatic speculation is the creation of a new species from a single ancestral species while living in the same region. That is why telling fish apart is complicated.

There are two species of grayling. The Arctic Grayling on the left is found in North America and Northern Asia and the European or Proper Grayling on the right is native to northern Europe. The fish have a similar look and there are color variations.

This is a book about catching grayling or more specifically how to find and catch all of the different grayling around the world. The book is organized by the different parts of the world where grayling can be found. The goal of the book is to identify the different subspecies, where they live and what it takes to catch them. I hope some people will pick up this book and decided to make a grayling trip. They are not the monster tackle busting fish like some of the trout but they have a beauty like no other fish. It is this beauty that I have come to appreciate.

They are easy to find in Europe and can be found in the rivers of northern Europe and throughout the British Isles. Proper Grayling are mostly river fish but there are lakes with grayling. Arctic Grayling are most abundant in the Far East. It is this region that has all of the different forms of grayling. It is possible to catch all subspecies in Russian and Mongolia. I spent a fair amount of time in both countries searching for grayling. Those travels allowed me to catch most of the different forms. There is an odd from of grayling in North Korea that is an isolated population of Amur Grayling. I mention this because if this fish were classified as a subspecies it would bring the total to fifteen. This fish is difficult to reach and is called the Yalu Grayling. This dwarf form of Amur Grayling is native to the headwaters of the Yalu River.

The grayling in North America and Europe are the fish that most people catch. They are the easiest to reach and range over fairly wide areas. Arctic Grayling in North America can be found from Hudson's Bay in Canada to the west coast. They are also native to Alaska and there is an isolated population in the Big Hole River of Montana. Grayling have been stocked in several states in the western United States. There was an isolated population in northern Michigan that is now extinct. Proper Grayling also go by the name of European Grayling and range from Scandinavia into northern Russia and most of the European Continent. They can also be found on the British Isles. They are very common in the countries of northern Europe and begin to decrease in the middle of the continent.

There are fourteen forms of grayling and most of them live in Russia. These two grayling are native to different parts of that country. The fish on the left is a Baikal White Grayling and the one on the right is an East Siberian Grayling. Both fish are among some of the largest grayling.

Catching the two main grayling species is not difficult. The challenge is trying to find and catch all of the subspecies. I was asked why I wanted to catch them all. The answer requires a story. When I began to study grayling it was difficult to find information. The information was out there but not in any one place. I wanted to put it all together in a book. Once I found all of the information I had to catch as many of the different types as I could. That was something that required a lot of travel and several years of fishing. But it was fishing and I didn't mind. The grayling search and the **Trout Adventures** series of books took me to places I never dreamed about seeing or fishing. I spent a lot of time in the Far East. That part of the world has wonderful fish and it became a great adventure. I found it to be an amazing place. There were mountains, volcanos and animals I had never seen. I found grayling and began to chip away at my goal of catching all of the grayling subspecies. I learned more about grayling as I fished my way around the world. Finding them was the challenge. That started in North America with several fishing trips to Wyoming and Montana. I later fished Canada and Alaska. North America was mostly river fishing but there were a few lakes. There were several unnamed lakes in Canada and Alaska plus Grebe Lake in Yellowstone National Park. After North America I went to the Far East. I began in Mongolia and on to Siberia and the Russian Far East. The final leg of the grayling journey was Europe. I started my search for Proper Grayling in the British Isles. Even though the fish in North Korea are not a separate subspecies I was disappointed that I could not get to the Yalu Grayling of North Korea. I didn't want to risk the possibility of being detained while I was there.

Fishing in Russia and Mongolia was the highlight of the grayling search. North America has beautiful fish and European Grayling were always a surprise when they turned up. The fish in Russia and Mongolia were big and beautiful. The North American fish began my grayling adventure and the Proper Grayling was the last species to be caught. In between those two fish were all of the other grayling forms and several years of travel in northern Asia.

It is possible that not all of the different types of grayling have been discovered. Travel is so difficult in the Far East that not all drainages have been fished or researched. I caught most of the different types of grayling and some were easy to identify while others were not. I caught grayling subspecies in areas where they hadn't previously been found and grayling that may be a new fish or a just color variation. It was exciting to catch something that has never been seen or discover a fish in a new area. Those experiences are discussed and it will be up to the researchers to decide the fate of all of the subspecies. This book will not resolve all of the problems with identification but will show what was caught and where all of the different grayling live. It is about finding grayling and the flies and techniques used in all of the different rivers and lakes. It is a search around the fringes of the Arctic Circle to find the magnificent grayling.

Arctic Grayling (Thymallus arcticus) are the most widespread. This fish its subspecies are worth working to find. The Proper Grayling (Thymallus thymallus) can be found in many European rivers and is probably caught more than any other type. The grayling that I found most interesting were the fish in Mongolia. They were big, beautiful and took a dry fly better than any other grayling. The Russian fish were also large and the grayling in the Amur River drainage were magnificent. As I fished my way through Mongolia and Russia my grayling total mounted and I had to begin think about the Proper Grayling. The Proper Grayling was the last on the list and it took a while to get to Europe. When I finally did get there my first stop was the British Isles. I spent some time fishing for grayling at each stop. I was excited to see the final piece of the grayling puzzle. The second river I fished in England was in the western moors and it was this area where I came face to face with a Proper Grayling. That grayling was the last part of my grayling odyssey and I was thrilled. I will continue to fish for grayling every chance I get. It is just something I like to do.

The Complete Book about Grayling provides the information needed to find and catch all of the grayling around the world. It is full of photographs and tips and identifies the best flies and rivers. The Grayling Plates provide pictures of all of the fourteen forms of grayling and the book shows color variations that have not yet been identified as a subspecies. Grayling are a special fish that that have an interesting past and need some help to continue to exist is some regions. They are the most elegant of fresh water fish.

Chapter 1 - North America

North America is where I learned about grayling. Where they lived, what they ate and even what looked like. The grayling of North America are Arctic Grayling they and range from the Hudson's Bay in northern Canada west into all of Alaska. They are northern fish so are only found in the northern parts of the Canadian Provinces as well as the Yukon Territory in Canada. There are several isolated populations in the continental United States. The only natural one is in the Big Hole River system in Montana. It is the last river population of grayling in the United States. There are several places in the United States where grayling were transplanted and have existed for many years. Wyoming has many places where grayling have existed for over

fifty years and Grebe Lake in Yellowstone is approaching a hundred year anniversary of the original grayling stocking. The problem with catching grayling in the lower forty-eight is that they are difficult to reach. There is a reason for that. Grayling live in the cleanest and most pristine water in the world. In the continental United States this is in the western mountains with little road access.

Some of the best places for grayling in North America are in Canada. The Yukon and Northwest Territories Have extensive grayling populations in most rivers and many lakes. The region around Yellowknife and Great

The largest grayling in North America are in Canada and Alaska. The western United States does have isolated populations.

Slave Lake are two areas where grayling are abundant. They range into northern British Columbia and are also in the northern areas of the other western provinces. Canada has many places with grayling and they are a favorite fish in the Yukon and western regions. These are the largest grayling in North America.

My search for grayling began in Yellowstone National Park. As the years went by I caught grayling in the Madison River as well as Grebe Lake in the Park. The largest grayling I caught in this area was a 16-inch fish that was part of the first grayling trip. That trip was the first of many grayling trips but it did require more thought. I had caught trout in the western mountains and had many opportunities to fly fish for Brown, Rainbow, Brook, and Cutthroat. I had also come to realize that there were whitefish in almost every western stream and they would take about any fly presented reasonably well. Grayling and whitefish are closely related and it seemed reasonable that grayling would take similar flies. These fish had my interest and I discovered that they existed in the high elevations of a few western States. I just had to figure out a way to catch one. I was a teenager and had to rely upon my parents to get me to the areas where they could be found. We were a fishing family but it would still take some planning. I began scheming to divert one of the western vacations into my first grayling trip. At this point in time I was at the mercy of my parents for western fishing trips. Mom and Dad still wanted all of us to take a summer vacation. In those days we generally spent a few days in Jackson Hole, Wyoming or West Yellowstone, Montana. I had fished in an around Yellowstone National Park several times and had found several good places for trout. My favorite river in the area was the Madison but the Snake was also very productive. It had been a long time since we had tried hiking into one of the backcountry lakes as a family and I sprung that proposal on everyone as a nice day trip in the mountains. I was surprised! They all liked the plan, or at least Dad said he would make the walk with me. We would fish the small lake in the Yellowstone high country. I was truly blessed. Everyone in the family liked to fish and was willing to walk three miles in the mountains to enjoy the experience. My mother did decide not to make that walk so it ended up

Arctic Grayling in North America are elegant fish. They are a shade of purple that makes them appear iridescent in the sunlight.

being a hike with Dad into Grebe Lake. I told Dad that there were grayling and Rainbow in the lake we would fish, but I didn't say that there was mostly grayling. Dad liked to catch Rainbow, and I wasn't sure how he would feel about spending the day catching a 12-inch fish that was related to whitefish. I couldn't wait for the trip, and was excited about the hike even as we drove out west. We were finally made it to West Yellowstone and eventually the day came for the walk into the lake.

We got up early that day and hit the trail. It was a sunny July day that became a fishing experience I have remembered all of my life. The trail was not awful, but did have some steep stretches and the waders I carried did get heavy. The effort was worth every step. Grebe Lake is not big and can be waded. The water around the edge of the lake is shallow with no drop-offs. The Lake is 156 acres and located at an elevation of 8000 feet. There are reeds and some shoreline vegetation, but that does not bother fly-casting. Wading out from shore did make it easier to make a back-cast.

I had done a lot of work and planning before our trip into Grebe Lake. We had Park fishing licenses, maps of the area, a copy of the park fishing regulations, and all of the dry flies and nymphs that should work. I had never seen a grayling except in pictures and was excited to try to catch one. I didn't have to wait long. On my second or third cast there was a hit and fish on. I was fishing a Stonefly Nymph with floating line and the fish took the fly shortly after it hit the water. The fish hit hard and put up a good fight. When I got the fish to the net I could see that it was a nice 14 or 15-inch Rainbow. What a disappointment! I had just walked for over two hours to catch Rainbow. I shrugged and made another cast. Just as quickly, there was another hit. This fish was not as big, and fought down in the water. It was a grayling! Not big, but that didn't matter. That 10-inch beauty was my first grayling and a fish I will always remember. The colors were magnificent. The purple and green on the body was beautiful, and irradiance on the dorsal fin and tail was something to see. Then there was the huge dorsal fin that made it look like a miniature sailfish. How could a fin that big be on such a small body? The only way to describe it is to say that it was a baby sailfish. I marveled at how beautiful that little fish was and slipped it back in the water. That fish was the beginning of a remarkable day. I caught grayling after grayling after grayling plus the occasional Rainbow. When the day was over I had caught over 60 grayling and three pretty nice Rainbow. I had a dilemma. I wanted to take a fish back to show everyone. This was in the 1960's and I didn't routinely take a camera with me as I do today. I kept the largest Grayling. It was 16-inches and would be one of the largest grayling I would ever catch in North America. I wrapped it in a plastic bag and put it in my pack. You were allowed to keep three fish in those days, but one grayling was all I wanted. I thought at the time that it would be nice to have a grayling mounted but 16-inches is not a very big fish.

I later found out that Grebe Lake has a history. In 1921 it was stocked with a Montana strain of Arctic Grayling. This form of Arctic Grayling was native to the Madison and Gibbon Rivers below Gibbon Falls within Yellowstone National Park. These fish are native to the area, and still exist in the Madison. Most lake dwelling grayling in the western United States can be traced to the Grebe Lake Grayling. There are two other lakes in the general area of Grebe that also have grayling. Wolf Lake to the west and Cascade Lake to the east also hold significant populations. The latest Park regulations require that all grayling be released.

When I moved to Alaska I came across more grayling. I worked for the Forest Service in the southeastern islands. This is a remote region that required a lot of travel by floatplane. I took a short floatplane ride with friend Paul Boyd one day into an unnamed lake. Paul had been there once before and knew that there was grayling in the lake and that they were not difficult to catch. Alaska is full of small lakes that contain grayling. The biggest problem is getting to them. Almost all of the lakes are either a long hike or a floatplane ride. The floatplane landed on the lake and taxied to the spillway where we began fishing. We cast back into the lake near the outlet and immediately began to catching fish. This was a day of catching and didn't require much skill. We caught many grayling that were all the same size at about 12-inches. This isolated lake received little pressure and the grayling seemed to take anything we wanted to cast at them. I lost count of the fish, but a lot of grayling were caught and released. It didn't seem to matter what we used, they would hit anything. Paul was fishing with a spinning rod and small spoon, and I had a fly rod with a stonefly nymph. We were both catching fish maybe not on every cast, but with almost every cast.

Grayling are distantly related to trout and are a special fish. The fish have a limited range in the United States because of their habitat requirements. They require cold and pristine water. As the last Ice Age receded in North America the grayling began to move north where the habitat best suited them. This left a few isolated populations in the continental United States with most of the fish in the northern areas of the continent. They are also susceptible to overfishing and that had an effect on the isolated populations. They were historically found in Montana and Michigan but one population has been eradicated and the other reduced. The grayling in Michigan have been extinct for many years and the fish in Montana were identified as endangered until recently. In the last few years the grayling in the Big Hole Valley of Montana have been removed from the endangered species list.

Grayling are common in Alaska and Canada but are not often the fish of choice in those areas. The trout in the far north are big fish and it is hard to past up Steelhead or big Rainbow for a grayling. I fished Alaska many times, but there was only one grayling trip out of several hundred fishing trips. The lakes in the southeastern islands are not that easy to find and require some knowledge of the area. It is a little easier to find grayling in the Alaska interior and the Kenai Peninsula. There are many lakes on the mainland of Alaska that have grayling and they are also common in several rivers. One of the better rivers is the Alagnak River in the Katmai Park and Preserve. The river has a huge population of bears and you will encounter bears if you fish this area and most other places in Alaska. Most people fish the river for salmon but there is a nice grayling population as well as several species of trout. The river is accessible from King Salmon which can be reached by commercial flights from Anchorage.

This is my favorite grayling picture for a couple of reasons. This is the only grayling I have ever caught with heart shaped spots and is also my largest North American grayling.

The last grayling trip I took in North America was to Meadow Lake in Wyoming. The road to Meadow Lake is four-wheel drive and it was needed. Maps help but it is easy to take a wrong turn. There were several turns and route decisions to make along the way and there were no signs. It was easy to take the wrong road. The last three miles of the road require four-wheel drive and is hopping from boulder to boulder. If you do choose the right fork you will eventually get to a prime grayling spot. The state of Wyoming uses Meadow Lake as a source lake for all of the grayling stocked in Wyoming. Needless to say it is a good lake for grayling. I spent most of one July day tubing Meadow Lake and caught as many grayling as I wanted to catch. The purple beauties in Meadow Lake were not hard to fool and fishing the lake from a tube got me to all of the best locations. Truthfully, one spot was as good as another because the grayling were definitely hitting. All of the fish I caught that day were in the 10-15 inch slot and it was fun to see that many grayling. It reminded me of the first grayling trip to Grebe Lake. Most of my success on Meadow Lake was with some form of stone fly nymph. When I fish lakes there is usually a lull in the fishing in the early afternoon, and that was true for Meadow Lake. I stopped fishing for a couple of hours and had a sandwich and drink. I waited too get back on the water until I saw fish rising.

I used a seven-foot rod with floating fly line and a ten-foot leader to fish Meadow Lake. The leader was six-pound test and I did cover as much water as possible in my power tube. Meadow Lake is not big, but at around 80-100 acres there is a lot of water to fish. There are also many acres of the lake that cannot be fished. It is not a deep lake and there was a lot of grass and vegetation that required fishing the open water to keep from getting grassed up. I caught most of the fish on the edge of the grass, but the largest fish hit in the middle of the lake far from any vegetation. This day was like the other grayling trips in North America and I was

amazed at the beauty of these purple sailfish. It was a good day on Meadow Lake and it is one of the better places that I have fished for grayling.

There have been several fishing trips where grayling have unexpectedly showed up. Grayling do exist in a few rivers in the United States and I have caught them in both the Big Hole River in Montana as well as the Madison River both inside and outside of Yellowstone National Park. None of the trips to these rivers was to catch grayling but they were a pleasant surprise. I caught nice grayling in the Madison River not far from the Grebe Lake Trailhead. I also caught two small

Meadow Lake, Wyoming has an excellent grayling population. These fish are used by the State to stock other waters. They lake is open to fishing but access is four-wheel drive.

grayling in the Madison not far from Ennis. This is probably my most surprising catch of these fish and I still can't explain how those two small grayling got that far down the Madison. The Big Hole River is identified by the State of Montana as the only river in the Continental United States with a native population of grayling and I have caught many grayling from the Big Hole. The difficulty is locating the fish in the river and the place where they exist one year will not produce fish the next.

My last fishing trip to the Big Hole did not produce any grayling and was generally not as productive as some of the other trips to the river. Water temperature has an effect on grayling and this was a warm summer with low water. I fished the river with Nephews Mark and Chris and we fished the river hard for a day. I wanted to fish the headwaters of the Big Hole but the low water made the headwaters difficult to find. There were many small streams and roads going everywhere as we drove toward the headwater. The roads were tracks in the field that lead to the mountains. Picking the right one was a crapshoot. These were four-wheel drive roads and my nephews didn't want to take the risk of getting in the middle of nowhere with a breakdown. Been there and done that but I was not as apprehensive about problems as the boys. I did go with the consensus and turned around to search for a spot downstream. We had gone over a nice sized fork of the Big Hole that was worth a try on the way out. The problem was that it was on private land and there was not a house within site to ask permission to fish. We could fish from around the bridge to see if anything was willing to take a fly. Mark and Chris didn't bother to get their fly rods out of the car but I am always ready to make a cast with a rod rigged and ready. I grabbed my rod and made a couple of quick casts downstream with no success, and turned for a few quick casts upstream and immediately got was a hit. I did miss the fish and muttered a few words under my breath. A few more casts brought another hit at about the same time we heard an interesting noise in some willow trees. The willows were thick and about12-15 feet high. There were no cattle in the area and I had heard that sound before in other parts of Montana and Alaska. It sounded like a black bear making bear sounds so it looked like it was time to leave. I did leave the area convinced that it was good grayling habitat.

The Big Hole River in Montana has the only population of native river grayling in the Continental United States. The numbers in the river have increased in recent years.

I decided to try some of the areas in the middle section of the river that had produced good Rainbow and a few grayling in the past. This section of river was slow and we moved on. The upper river around Wisdom was also slow fishing but produced a few whitefish and several good Rainbows. I knew something was wrong, because there were not many people fishing the river. That is always a tip. We did find more action when we moved to the faster water toward Wise River, but more action in this case meant big whitefish. This is one of the few times that it was nice to see whitefish. After spending several hours catching a few fish, it was good to get into some nice fish and fast action. The water was fast, the fish were big, and it was fun to see everyone having line zip from their reel. It was a disappointing day for grayling.

Alaska and the north region of the western Provinces of Canada have the best grayling fishing in North America. The Yukon, Northwest Territories and Nunavut Provinces all contact grayling in most rivers. They also exist in the most northern regions of Manitoba, Saskatchewan, Alberta and extreme northern British Columbia. Cold water is the key to finding Arctic Grayling and is where they exist. In Canada this is north of the 55th parallel. Places that have a good reputation for grayling in Canada are Great Slave Lake and Beaulieu River in the Northwest Territories, Lake Teenah, Drury Lake and the Kathleen River, Yukon. There are also many rivers in northern Saskatchewan such as the Fond du Lac.

The North American fish do hold a special place in my heart, and I will make other trips to catch them. The grayling trip that created my passion for grayling was the trip to Grebe Lake. There have been trips where I caught more grayling and many trips where I caught bigger fish but this was the best day of fishing I have ever had. Catching grayling with my Dad was a great memory. Dad is gone and he left me a legacy of fishing, love of the out-of-doors and of animals. I want to go back to Grebe Lake to relive that memory someday. The walk into Grebe Lake is pleasant and I can think about fishing with Dad. He was willing to take a walk with me those years ago to a lake he knew nothing about for a fish he had never heard of. Being with him that day is a great memory and sharing the experience of my first grayling trip with him is hard to describe. The next trip I will probably be alone and will try to see how the grayling have fared over the years. This time I will take a tube and cover a lot more of the lake than I did on the first trip. It should be another good day of fishing.

Chapter 2 - Searching Mongolia for Grayling

During my search for information I learned that most of different types of Arctic Grayling live in Siberia and Mongolia. I spent several weeks fishing the rivers of Mongolia. I found beautiful grayling and fish that I could not identify. The country became one of my favorites as I worked my way around the northern rivers. Grayling were in every river and the country had some of the most colorful grayling I had seen. I discovered an enchanting land with excellent grayling fishing. I started with a trip to the northeast and a float down the Onon River. Most trips were not exclusively for grayling but I spent time fishing for grayling on each trip. I did make one grayling trip but even then I caught some nice trout. All of my fishing friends thought it was strange that I would travel that far to fish for grayling. It was during those conversations that I realized most people don't have an appreciation for one of the most magnificent cold water fish. I suppose it is because they are related to whitefish and are not trout. They are special and my grayling adventure in Mongolia was the start of a search for some of the most magnificent fish in the Arctic.

Mongolia is well known as one of the best places to catch Taimen and Lenok but grayling are the most common fish. Not much has been written about their abundance in Mongolia or where they can be found. I decided to try to change that. My first Mongolian trip was to the Onon River in the northeast. I fished for trout during the day and grayling in the evening. That strategy worked but I was

Mongolia has the most colorful grayling I was able to find. I never did get used to the rainbow fish I found in that wonderful country.

disappointed because all of the grayling I caught were small. The Onon had Amur Grayling that are one of several forms of grayling found in that drainage. I knew there were larger grayling in Mongolia and began to look for other grayling rivers. That search took me around the country and allowed me to discover more than I anticipated.

The topography in Mongolia is different than any place I have fished. It has one of the largest deserts in the world in the south, mountains in the north, and in-between are the Mongolian steppes. The Gobi Desert is one of the driest areas in the world and even camels find it too dry to live in the southern part of this vast desert. The middle of the country has the largest steppes in the world. Steppes are areas where there is not enough water for trees but enough rainfall for grass. It is the northern part of the country that has all of the rivers and mountains. A transition area exists between the steppes and mountains where foothills have both trees and grass.

There are three major drainages in Mongolia and each one has several different types of grayling. The Onon River is a tributary of the Amur River that is part of the Pacific drainage. This river is located in northeast Mongolia. The Amur system has many species of fish that are unique to this vast drainage area. The Selenge River flows into Lake Baikal, Siberia and represents the headwaters of the Yenisei River. This system drains into the Arctic Ocean. The western drainage is comprised of the rivers that flow into what is called the Great Lakes Depression. The depression is an area in western Mongolia where several rivers terminate in a lakes region. All three drainages are isolated from each other and

The Eg River is the outflow of Lake Khovsgol and is one of the best grayling rivers in the country.

different grayling forms have developed in each drainage. There are five grayling subspecies native to Mongolia and two other forms that are shared with Russia. The two Russian fish are both found in the Selenge drainage. To catch all of the different Mongolian grayling each of the three drainages has to be fished. The five grayling native to Mongolia are: Khovsgol Black Grayling (*Thymallus arcticus nigrescens*), Mongolia Grayling (*Thymallus arcticus brevirostris*), Arctic Grayling (*thymallus arcticus*), Amur Grayling (*Thymallus arcticus grubii*) and the Yellowtail Grayling (*Thymallus arcticus svetovidovi*). The Amur Grayling occurs in Russian as well as Mongolia as does the Yellowtail Grayling (*Thymallus arcticus svetovidovi*). Baikal Black Grayling (*Thymallus arcticus baicalensis*) and Baikal White Grayling (*Thymallus arcticus brevipianis*) are Russian fish that wander into Mongolia. Mongolian Grayling can be found in two forms (regular sized and dwarf) in the western rivers.

There are some that would ask "Why bother"? When I fished North America I went out of the way to catch all of the forms of Cutthroat Trout. The United Sates has gone to great lengths to help preserve and in some cases restore some of the Cutthroat subspecies that have seen their numbers reduced. Unfortunately, some have been eradicated. Grayling in some parts of the world have suffered the same plight. I think it is important that all of the forms of grayling be identified to insure that all remain healthy. Identifying all grayling subspecies is the only way to insure that each survives. The study of grayling in Mongolia and Siberia is incomplete. That makes fishing for grayling in these parts of the world interesting. I studied all of the information I could about grayling in Mongolia. Studies indicate that a thorough search of Mongolian rivers for grayling and other fish has not been completed. I caught grayling that I could not identify as well as subspecies from rivers where they had not previously been found.

There is much to be learned about the grayling in Mongolia but one thing is known. Most of the grayling in Mongolia are big fish. My first grayling experience on the Onon River was the only time I caught any small fish. All of the other rivers had some of the largest grayling I have seen. The largest I caught weighted about six pounds and several fish were able to take me into the backing on the reel.

There were many color variations. Both of these fish are an Arctic Grayling subspecies, but do not have typical coloration. Both were caught in the Eg River.

The Selenge River System is the largest in Mongolia and is located in the northcentral part of the country. It included Lake Khovsgol which is the largest lake in Mongolia and several major rivers. Baikal Black Grayling (*Thymallus arcticus baicalensis*) are the most common grayling in this drainage but there are other subspecies. One of the most interesting is the Khovsgol Black Grayling (Thymallus arcticus nigrescens) that can only found in Lake Khovsgol. Baikal White Grayling (*Thymallus arcticus brevipinnis*) and Arctic Grayling (*Thymallus arcticus*) exist in some rivers. Yellowtail Grayling are close to Lake Khovsgol but difficult to reach. This grayling is found in the rivers of the Darkhat Depression that are part of the headwaters of the Yenisei River. There are two grayling that require fishing other drainages. Mongolian Grayling (*Thymallus arcticus brevirostris*) require fishing the rivers of the Great Lakes Basin and Amur Grayling (*Thymallus arcticus grubii*) are found in the Onon River. The only way to get to the rivers with heavy concentrations of grayling was to search the northern rivers. I set up a three week period in late June one year to search for Mongolia grayling.

I knew I would have to make special arrangements to trek around the country by myself. I made some contacts and arranged for a driver and interpreter to go with me to the north. The northern regions are somewhat accessible and there are commercial flights to some villages. The airplanes vary in size but all are turboprops. The important part of the grayling trip was finding a 4x4 to get to the rivers. It takes several hours of driving to reach the rivers from any rural airport. The trip started with a flight from Ulaanbaatar to Moron. The flight to Moron was good and it was a beautiful day. There is always some apprehension with local flights because there are days when the planes don't fly. There is a schedule and usually the flight will happen on the day it is scheduled. There are some days the planes just don't fly. Rain is usually not the issue but wind will stop all flights. I did have to wait six hours for a flight out of Moron and thought I would have to spend the night. That didn't happen but it did give me time to check out about the village. I spent much of the day walking around and could have found a place to stay. I learned during my Far East travels that it pays to be flexible.

It does take planning to travel to the Mongolian Rivers. In some parts of the country charter flights are needed to land in a field close to the river. Other rivers can be reached by a fly and drive system using local airlines. Travel to the rivers is a long drive from any place the planes can land.

Northern Mongolia gets more rain than the rest of the country. Every trip I took had a few days of rain. That didn't bother the fishing but it did make for cold days. I was there during the summer in June-August and the mornings were always cool. It was typical to start the day with temperatures in the thirties and on several days there was frost. Ulaanbaatar has the coldest average annual temperature of any capital in the world. It is a cold county. I always had jackets, sweatshirts and raingear on every trip. The mountains around Lake Khovsgol had snow in July and all of the water in the far north was some of the coldest water I have experienced.

The trip from Moron to the western mountains took about six hours in a Land Rover. I was with several other fishermen on the first leg of the journey but we would part company after a couple of days. They would float down the Delger River and I would go on to other rivers by vehicle. My travels would eventually take me to Lake Khovsgol as I fished my way around the region. The backcountry in this area was made up of rolling hills and eventually mountains. The Mongolian drivers were great. They knew where they were going and just drove to a place on the river. The Delger is in the mountains and the closer we got to the river the rougher the road and terrain became. The last few miles required rock hopping, mud, and steep side slopes. We stopped on a cliff that overlooked a large meandering river. This was our campsite for the first night. I walked to the river after we got the gear out of the vehicles.

I liked the looks of the Delger and saw fish rising close to shore. I went back to the pile of gear and got my duffle out for a quick change. It took me about five minutes to rig up and get back to the river. I cast an Adams to the rising fish and there was an immediate strike. After a short fight I was able to see my first Delger grayling. It was not a big fish but was a nice grayling that looked similar to the fish in North America. I decided it was an Arctic Grayling and took a few pictures before I slide the fish back into the water. I enjoyed the days on the Delger and caught many grayling. Arctic and Baikal While Grayling seemed to be the most common in the section I fished but there were also Baikal Black Grayling. Lenok were everywhere and was the most common fish caught. I modified some Clouser flies to make them smaller in an effort to attract more large grayling. The modification caught many large Lenok and some nice grayling. There are Taimen in the Delger but I didn't spend any tine fishing for Taimen. I was after grayling. There were a few areas where fishing was slow but in most sections there was plenty of action. The other people on the float were fishing for Taimen and did not catch any the two days I floated with them. The Delger was productive for grayling and I caught several big fish. The largest was a little over three pounds. I thought that was a nice grayling but the bigger ones came later.

It was when I left the Delger that trip became interesting. My friend Hishgee had agreed to be my guide and interpreter for the rest of the trip. She was familiar with the area and had worked for five years in the northern village of Khatgal. Khatgal is on the south end of Lake Khovsgol and is the only village in the area. Ganchulun was our driver. He used to be a herder and knew the area like the back of his hand. His sense of direction and knowledge was amazing. He raised horses and his horses had won the National Horse Race several times. He did not speak much English but was pleasant to be around. He was much more than a driver. Hishgee and Ganchulun would talk about where we should go and we would be off. There are few roads and it was nice to be with someone that knew the area. I was in good company with people that knew what I was after and took me everywhere. The grayling search was more than I imagined and turned out to be my favorite trips. We found different rivers and drove all over the north. On our way back

These markers identify the graves of the relatives of Chinggis Khaan. He was from this northern region.

from the Delger River we drove through the northern foothills. The first part of the trip was the drive out of the Delger Valley. The canyon walls were steep and the road fell straight up or down in some stretches. It was an interesting start to an interesting day. After about four hours we came to several piles of rock and what looked like a monument. We stopped and everyone got out. I ask Hishgee about the large piles of stone and the markers. She took me over to one of the markers and said that the markers were burial stones for the descendants of Chinggis Khaan. They had been in this place for hundreds of years and the area was considered a scared. There were three very tall monuments with a circle of rocks around each of them. It was then that we went to the large pile of stones where my Mongolian education took a surprising turn. I was introduced to Shamanism. It is an ancient religion in northern Asia that believes in a spiritual relationship between nature and people. The large pile of stones was a scared rock cairn called an Oboo. It was home to the local mountain spirit and we stopped to pay respect to the spirit. We paid respect by walking around the Oboo three times and placing another rock on the pile. In return for our respect the mountain spirit would grant us safe journey and Wind Horse. Wind Horse is the symbol for prosperity. We spent about thirty minutes at this scared placed and then continued our journey. Hishgee told me many stories about Mongolia as we traveled and I learned about the country. My journey took me to places few foreigners have seen and helped me understand Mongolian life.

I asked Hishgee about Shamanism and what she thought about the ancient religion. She told me a story about her friend that worked in an office in Ulaanbaatar. She had known this lady all of her life and her friend was like most of the young people in the Mongolian capital. But a few years ago the friend was visited by a spirit. These spirits select someone to become a Shaman. A Shaman is a medium that allows the spirit world to deal with the world of people. This visit changed her friend's life forever. A spirit began speaking through her in his native language that was several hundred years old. An interpreter had to be brought in to identify what was being said. Over the next two years two other spirits began to speak through this woman. Hishgee heard about what her friend was going through and decided that she had to see her. Her visit was a revelation as the three spirits came to speak to her and spoke in their ancient voices. The strange voices used by her friend raised many questions. The visit left Hishgee with a feeling that the ancient religion may be valid. We had more conservations during our time together and she taught me how the Mongolians feel and care for the land.   I pondered the mountain spirits and Shamanism as we turned off a good road on a trail to the Eg River.

Not many people fish the Eg except for the herders that live along its banks. It became one of my favorite rivers. It was just large enough to hold big fish. The day was cold and rainy so I pulled on my rain gear and grabbed my small rod.   There was a herder nearby that watched me get ready to fish. The nice thing about fishing Mongolia was that all rivers are open for fishing. All it takes is a license. We drove downriver and came to a rocky area that I didn't think we could cross. I had my hand on the door ready to get out when Ganchulun put the Land Rover in low and started over the rocks. We squeezed through the tight section where it seemed like we were upside down once or twice. I came to respect his judgment on driving and places to fish. He really knew the Eg and everywhere we fished was good. We got to the river late in the day and I was able to catch several grayling. I found a pool with several boulders that looked like a grayling haven. I started catching nice grayling immediately and one of the largest fish was marked a differently. It was a big Baikal Black Grayling with different colors. When I first looked at it I thought it was a Yellowtail Grayling. Those fish were not in the Eg so I took several pictures for later review. I was encouraged to see a different looking fish. It was at least three pounds fish and I was well on my way to catching the grayling of Mongolia.

The next way was an introduction to one of the rarest and most unique fish in the world. Khosvgol Black Grayling are native to the Lake for which they are named and only leave the lake to spawn. Mongolia is not a fishing culture and people seldom eat fish. The exception is Black Grayling. People have discovered how to catch them in the winter with nets through the ice. This system is having an impact of grayling numbers and there is also illegal netting on some of the inlet streams during spawning. Smoked grayling has become a delicacy in northern Mongolia. We tried to buy some smoked grayling at the Khatgal stores but there had been a run on smoked grayling and all had been sold.

Black Grayling were spawning during the time I was there and I wanted to see streams choked with grayling. Our first trip would be to the "River that Never Freezes" on the western side of the lake. The "River that Never Freezes" is a sacred place to the local Mongolians. The mountain spirits have blessed this river with the ability to stay open all year and its waters have special powers. Anyone that drinks the water and eats a fish from the river will have good health for the year. If that is done three years in a row, good health will be received for a lifetime. The spawn had already occurred in the "River that Never Freezes" and try as I might I could not catch any fish. During the long drive back to Khatgal we also stopped and visited the Reindeer People. These mountain people raise reindeer for their only income and are recognized as a separate culture. They were very kind and invited us into their tents. These tents were not the Gers used by the herders in much of the north. Reindeer People live in what we would call teepees. I did not

The "River that Never Freezes" is a long drive up the west side of Lake Khovsgol. The river has special meaning to Mongolians.

get the Mongolian word for their tents but they were big and several people could fit inside. They also had some of the biggest dogs I have seen. I was told that they were wolf dogs and protected the reindeer from wolves. The reindeer are shackled at night so they do not wander far from the protection of the dogs. It was an interesting day that was a bust for fishing. I had discovered that the Black Grayling spawn was over in the northern inlets. If that was true in the rest of the lake it was going to be a lot more difficult to catch some of these different looking grayling.

The next day was voting day in Mongolia and a new parliament and president were to be elected. I found that out when we passed a small building that had horses, trail bikes, and cars all around it. I asked what was going on and was told that all of the people in the area were voting. We had already driven a long way and this small building was in the middle of nowhere. It was surprising to see so many people in one place. We were getting close to the Russian border and passed several vehicles with border patrol officers. I had seen them in northeastern Mongolia but the patrol was different in this area. Here they had four-wheel drive vehicles and many more officers. In the east, the patrol used horses and patrolled an area alone. The drive up the east side of the lake was different then my experience the day before. The west side had forests with hills close to the lake shore. The east side was open fields with large herds of goats and sheep. The road steadily got worse as we drove up the shoreline. We came to a small stream and fish scattered as we drove across. They were grayling and the spawn was not over in this part of the lake. We followed this small stream and found where it emptied into the lake.

I began fishing the stream inlet where it entered the lake. I didn't see any fish trying to enter the stream so suggested we move upstream. We followed the stream into the middle of a yak herd and there were grayling everywhere. I put on a small caddis nymph and starting casting. There was not much interest. It seemed that this fish had other things on their mind. I kept casting and was finally able to hook a fish. My first Black Grayling. I was thrilled to see one and thought back to the words of a guide who had fished area. He said that they were ugly fish. I looked at the fish and decided it was different but not ugly. I fished for about two hours on that small stream and lost track of the number of fish that I caught. I did find out that the best way to catch them was to use a #14-16 Adams and fish it as a wet fly. I got many strikes as the fly swung across the current just below the surface and more by leaving the fly in the water at the end of the drift. I had caught enough fish by early

The blue rimmed eyes and mouth of the Khovsgol Black Grayling are unique. These dark fish have a purple glow in the right light.

afternoon and decided it was time to head for the Eg. There would be some big Lenok as well as several different types of grayling to complete the day. Ganchulun made a turn toward the mountains and I was in for a surprise. He wanted to show me his racehorses that were to race in the National Horse Race next month. We drove up to a hitching rail where six horses were tied. I raise horses so I decided to get a closer look. I discovered several trips before that Mongolian horses are skittish and I approached very slowly from a direction where they could all see me. It didn't matter. None of them wanted anything to do with me. After about ten minutes I was able to put my hand on one. It was a breakthrough but as soon as I moved he jumped straight sideways and ended up a couple of feet from my hand. I gave up trying to make Mongolian horse friends and walked back to Hishgee. She said that we had been invited into the trainer's germ for sweet cakes and goat milk tea. We all headed for the Ger. The men talked horses long enough for me to have two cups of tea and several sweet cakes. It was a nice break.

I took a quick inventory of the grayling I had caught as we drove to the Eg. I looked through the pictures on my camera and was able to identify Baikal White Grayling, Baikal Black Grayling, Arctic Grayling, Mongolian Grayling, and Khovsgol Black Grayling. I had caught Amur Grayling from an earlier trip. I was in pretty good shape. There were many fish on the camera that were not typical. The Yellow Grayling that I had caught earlier in the Eg was either another type of grayling or a color variation and some of the grayling I caught in the Delger were also different. Needless to say there were lots of different grayling and I couldn't wait for some more time on the river. I was able to catch two large Lenok and several more grayling to finish out the day. The next day was cold and rainy and I fished a different section of the Eg. It was raining hard and I told everyone to stay in the land rover while I fished. The fishing was great and I caught many fish by skidding a big hopper along the surface.

The Mongolian Grayling in the first picture does resemble the Siberian Grayling in the second picture. Finding these fish were part of the challenge of searching Mongolia for grayling. The reward was beautiful fish.

All of the northern rivers were excellent for grayling. I liked the Eg because it seemed to have the largest fish and many different forms. I expected to see Arctic Grayling in the northern rivers but was surprised to find Baikal Black and White Grayling. I consider the Mongolian and Yellowtail Grayling the most difficult to catch. Not because they are hard to fool but because they are both difficult to reach. Getting to them is a challenge. Mongolian Grayling are the largest of all of the Grayling subspecies. These fish are relic grayling that were left landlocked after the Tertiary geologic period and only inhabit the rivers in the western part of the country. These rivers do not have the variety of fish as other Mongolian rivers but they do have Mongolian Grayling. I was able to catch a few Mongolian Grayling but it would have been much easier to fly further west and fish the rivers in Dzavhan Provence. The problem with that was that it would have taken several days and there was only one grayling type to catch. I was satisfied with the success in the rivers I fished. There are some rivers in the west where grayling are the only fish. Mongolian Grayling (*Thymallus arcticus brevirostris*) exist in a small or dwarf form as well as the standard or large size. The fish in the Great Lakes Basin are not as colorful as those in the Selenge drainage but like all grayling they have a certain beauty.

Siberian Grayling in this part of the world are Arctic Grayling by another name. There are a few isolated populations in Mongolia. They were in several rivers and I probably caught six or seven on the grayling trip. The rivers I fished in northern Mongolia are in the arctic drainage and I had expected to see Arctic Grayling. They were not as abundant as I thought they would be. The fish I caught were in the headwater streams. All of the northern rivers in the middle of the country are part of the Selenge Drainage and I guess I should have expected Baikal White and Black Grayling. The Selenge is the main inflow into Lake Baikal and those grayling do leave the lake. Those two forms were in Mongolia.

Yellowtail Grayling are also known as Upper Yenisei Grayling and can be found in the rivers of the Darkhat Depression.

The Darkhat Depression is across the Russian border in Mongolia and is just west of Lake Khovsgol. The depression is home to one of the most recently discovered grayling subspecies. The rivers in the depression are headwaters of the Yenisei River. These headwater rivers are home to a grayling form discovered in 2006. Yellowtail Grayling (*Thymallus arcticus svetovidovi*) have a limited range that includes the rivers in the depression and a few rivers across the border in Siberia. These grayling are also known as Upper Yenisei Grayling but the more popular Yellowtail Grayling is more common. The rivers in Mongolia with Yellowtail are the Sharga Gol River and the Shishkid Gol River. These may be headwaters but they are not small streams. The depression allows them to collect water quickly and they are medium sized rivers early in the depression. There is a ferry that allows travel across Shishkid Gol and is part of the experience of reaching this remote region.

Onon River in the northeast is home to Amur Grayling. As more grayling were discovered in the Amur drainage it has become more difficult to keep all of the Amur grayling straight. There are Upper Amur Grayling as well as Lower Amur Grayling in the Russian Far East. See the grayling in Siberia and the Russian Far East for a full explanation of all grayling in the Amur drainage. I was able to catch several small grayling each evening during my time on the Onon River. They were plentiful next to the bank. I was surprised that they were not large fish and turned out to be the smallest of all the Mongolian grayling I caught. They were my first grayling in Mongolia and I credit them for getting me excited to search for the other types.

Searching Mongolia for grayling was one of the greatest adventures I have had. It was amazed at all of the different types of grayling and it was exciting to find some I couldn't identify. I think several new subspecies will be found in Mongolia when more rivers are sampled. There were many different looking grayling that made me curious about their origin. The Black Grayling of Lake Khovsgol are a special fish. They were not ugly as I had been told but are the most unique and different grayling of all I have found. I had never seen a river full of grayling like I experienced fishing the inlets of Lake Khovsgol. That is the most lasting memory I have about Mongolia grayling.

I didn't know what to expect when I began the search for Mongolia grayling. I discovered new friends as well as different grayling. There are many places around the world to catch these wonderful fish. Mongolia has some of the largest and most colorful of all grayling. It has some of the best grayling fishing in the world.

Chapter 3 - Grayling of Siberia

Siberia is a vast area in northern Russia that has three of the largest rivers in the world. All of these massive rivers flow into the Arctic Ocean and all of them have grayling. Siberia has more grayling than any other region in the world and along with the Russian Far East has more

Siberia geographically is all of the area in Russia east of the Ural Mountains. It represents over ten percent of the world's landmass. Russia divides this region into Siberia and another area on the coast of the North Pacific called the Russian Far East.

Map - The World Factbook

forms of grayling than the rest of the world combined. The eastern part of Russian is the grayling capital of the world. The three major drainages that flow into the Arctic Ocean contain different grayling. The Lena, Yenisei and Ob Rivers begin in the mountains of southern Siberia and flow north. A fourth system begins in Mongolia, flows through a portion of Siberia and terminates at the Pacific Ocean in a region known as the Russian Far East. The Amur River system is the largest drainage in Russian to flow into the Pacific.

There are seven forms of grayling found in Siberia: Arctic Grayling (*Thymallus arcticus*), Baikal Black Grayling (*Thymallus arcticus baicalensis*), Baikal White Grayling (*Thymallus arcticus brevipianis*), Upper Yenisei Grayling (*Thymallus arcticus svetovidovi*), Upper Lena Grayling (*Thymallus arcticus lenensis*), East Siberia Grayling (*Thymallus arcticus pallasii*) and the Amur Grayling (*Thymallus arcticus grubii*). Grayling in Siberia are distributed north and south. Five of these grayling live in southern Siberia while the other two tend to be more northern fish. All of these fish except the East Siberian Grayling and Upper Lean Grayling can also be found in Mongolia.

Baikal White and Baikal Black Grayling are native to Lake Baikal and are found in many rivers in the area. Baikal is the largest lake in the world and grayling are the most abundant fish in the lake. Both of the Baikal forms travel into Mongolia and can be found in the Selenge River system. The Upper Yenisei Grayling and the Amur Grayling are also found in both countries. The Upper Lena Grayling are fairly widespread, but are most common around the north end of Lake Baikal. There are several rivers and lakes in this area where they can be found. There are also a few rivers closer to the Arctic Ocean with this form of grayling. Three grayling in southern Siberia are found in specific drainages within the region. Amur Grayling and Upper Amur Grayling inhabit the Amur River and all tributaries from the headwaters to the point where the Bureya River enters the Amur. The Upper Yenisei Grayling or Yellowtail Grayling is found in a local area on the Mongolia/Siberia border known as the Darkhat Depression. There

The Angara River flows through Irkutsk and is fished heavily for grayling and Lenok Trout. It is a major river and the only outflow of Lake Baikal. There are several dams on the Angara before it reaches the Yenisei.

are several rivers in the depression where these fish are common. East Siberian Grayling is a northern fish found in the Lena and Yenisei drainages close to the Arctic Ocean. Arctic or Siberian Grayling are also more common in the northern rivers. Baikal Black Grayling are the most common grayling in this region.

One of the better places to reach some of the rivers is Irkutsk. It is fairly large city in southern Siberia with a good airport and daily flights. It is close to Lake Baikal and there are four or Five types of grayling within reach of Irkutsk. I flew to Irkutsk from Mongolia late one evening and the next morning was a surprise. I woke up in the land of OZ. Irkutsk was not what I expected! I am not sure what I expected but whatever it was this was not it. Siberia had always brought thoughts of isolation, snow, and cold weather but this Siberia was none of that. Irkutsk was beautiful. This there was grass, flowers, and people enjoying being outside. It was so different than what I expected I took an early walk to take in the surroundings.

I spent the morning exploring the city and eventually found the Angara River. This river is the only outlet from Lake Baikal and is a big river when it leaves the lake. The Angara is the largest tributary of one of the largest rivers in the world - the Yenisei. The river appeared to be a popular fishing spot. There were many Russians fishing along its banks as well as from boats. I stopped and watched them as I walked along the bank. Most had a bucket or basket with grayling and occasionally there was a Lenok Trout. The fishing technique being used by the Russian fishermen was different. It was a combination casting/fly system that made me curious. I got a closer look later in the trip.

I watched for a while and walked into an area with many magnificent churches. I knew enough about Russia to know that most Russians belonged to the Russian Orthodox Church. All of the churches were beautiful and the architecture was ornate with much gold leaf. I walked on and became fascinated with the city and its people. Irkutsk was filled with people that liked getting outside and having fun. There weren't many people that spoke English so I got by with a lot of pointing and a few basic Russian words. It was time to figure out how to get to Lake Baikal. I went back to the hotel and ask if there was a way to get to Lake Baikal. I was told that most people take the bus that runs several times a day between Irkutsk and Listvyanka. Listvyanka is a village on the west shore of the lake and a place where I thought it might be possible to get a boat. Bank fishing can be done along the lake but fishing the largest lake in the world from the bank seemed a little iffy. The road ends just passed Listvyanka and I knew that all of the areas with good access were heavily fished. I thought it would be better to find a place with few

people. I needed a boat. After more discussion with the hotel, I did find someone to drive me to Listvyanka. Unfortunately, his English was about like my Russian so we had an interesting time together. He was willing and fun and I learned many things as he helped me along.

Listvyanka was full of open markets with items for tourists. Few people spoke English and I had to point at an article to get the price. I went to Baikal several days in a row and it took some time to find a boat and arrange fishing. The people that did speak English said that the best fishing was on

Fishing the largest lake in the world required a large boat and a different technique. I wasn't prepared for the size of the boat or the type of fishing.

the north end of the lake. To get to the north end was a two or three day boat trip. I didn't want to take that much time so looked for other alternatives. I checked out possibilities as we drove around the village and noticed a dock with several large boats at the west end of town. I decided to go to the dock and talk with the boat captains as best I could. Close to the dock was a small building that said in English "Boats." I stopped to see if they could help. There were two people talking with a couple in Russian. I looked around the office and noticed a stack of maps that said tourist office on the top line. That was encouraging and I wondered if they would be able to direct me to a fishing boat. I ask if anyone spoke English. The lady behind the counter motioned to a young man outside and he came in to speak to me. I explained that I wanted to get a boat to fish around lake. He said that he would have to go speak to the captains on the dock to see if someone was available. He asked me to wait and was gone for a while. He came back in about twenty minutes and said that one of the boats was available and went on to explain that all of the boats were set up for many fishermen. It was unusual to have just one. I wasn't sure what that meant so I went down to the dock to see just what I was getting into. It was a short distance to the dock and as I gazed at the boats I understood what my young Russian friend was saying. All of the boats were about forty feet long and were twin screw, steel hulled vessels. I have fished many places and had seen this type of boat on the oceans where there were used as party fishing boats. It wasn't what I expected but this was the largest lake in the world and I probably should have considered that there would be large vessels on the water. I wanted to fish the lake and said this boat would be fine. I had learned to be open to anything on my travels in the Far East and this adventure was unfolding before my eyes. The captain spoke no English so I shook his hand and said "thank you" in Russian. My next though was how I was going to fly fish from this massive boat. I would figure that out latter and went back to the car for my fishing gear. It was an overcast day and I noticed that the captain was wearing a heavy parka. I was August but the wind was blowing and the temperature was about forty degrees. I knew

Fishing technique was different in Lake Baikal. The bow of this boat is on shore and the motor is close to full power. The first time I saw this I wasn't sure what was happening.

that it would be colder on the lake. I was right and the breeze felt much colder when we got underway. The boat was under full power heading toward the north end of the lake and it seemed to be getting colder by the minute. I put on every piece of clothing I had brought with me. Jacket, raincoat, and gloves all helped keep me a little warmer. Even when we slowed down it didn't get any warmer. I could see my breath. It was the middle of the morning in August and the temperature had to be in the thirties. I was shivering in the warmest part of summer and wondered what a Siberian winter was like. I shook my head and turned my attention back to the boat. We began to slow down and I looked at the shoreline. There were cliffs and a rocky beach. I thought we would anchor some distance from shore and I would cast to the beach. That was not the way that the Russians fish Baikal. The captain pointed the boat toward the rocks and gave it some power. I watched as the bow hit the rocks and the nose became imbedded. This was one way to keep the boat in position. I made a cast over the side. The captain came back and waved his hand back and worth and said "Nyet, nyet". I knew that this meant no and realized that he had something else in mind. He went back to the wheelhouse and set the engines on high RPM's. We were beached with the engines whining at close to full revolution throwing a wake of about 300 feet. He pointed to the prop wash and said "fish". We had just created our own Baikal River and were going to fish this man-created stream. He said several things in Russian and I began to understand what was going on. The fish come to the prop wash to pick up all of the bottom insects that get carried out into the lake.

There were several rods on the boat and I motioned for the captain to get a rod and fish with me. I ask him if he was a good fisherman and he said "nyet." The rods used Russian rods and reels were different. They looked somewhat like fly rods with a large arbor reel but are used like casting rods. They are fished with flies, weights, and floats. The reels have several hundred yards of line and are free spooling so they can be thrown a long way. The Russians generally make very long casts and let the current carry the float downstream. After a long drift the flies are reeled in. There are usually 2-3 flies below the float. The weight is placed below the flies. It is an interesting rig and does catch fish. The flies used by the Russians are very small in size 16-22 and usually scuds or nymphs. I did see several Russians fishing with only a gold bead and gold hook. The majority of fish caught were grayling but there were a few Lenok that they call Siberian Trout. I did see some Omul (a small whitefish) in some of the streams and Lake Baikal. These fish are harvested in great numbers by commercial fisherman on Baikal and are available in most of the restaurants. The fish market is in the middle of Listvyanka had smoked Omul and that is what many Russians have for lunch.

The signature fish around Lake Baikal is the fish on the right. The Baikal Black Grayling is common in the lake and surrounding rivers. The fish on the left is the Baikal White Grayling and is not as common but is occasionally caught. Both fish are a large form of grayling.

The captain got out a couple of boxes of flies and picked up one of the longer rods. He rigged up a rod as I made my first cast into the wash. This may have been the most interesting fishing experience I have ever had. Everything I found in Siberia was different and this day was off to a promising start. I was fishing sinking tip fly line and cast out of the main current and let the line feed out my reel until the end of the backing. That was over 200 yards of line and covered much of the wash. After a few casts I got a hard hit and lost a fish. I kept casting and got another hit and this time I was able to see the fish. It was a grayling. I wondered how we were going to get the fish the five or six feet up to the deck. I played the fish for a little while and was ready to bring him over the side. It was about then that the Captain produced a net and I got a look at a nice Baikal Black Grayling. I had caught several in Mongolia but it was nice to catch one in Baikal. I dropped him over the side. Throwing the fish back brought several words from the captain. I had forgotten that Russians keep all fish and that catch and release is not practiced. I tried to explain that I didn't keep any of the fish but I was sure he didn't understand. I motioned for him to get his rod and we continued to fish. It was challenging to fish the prop wash because of all of the vegetation that the propellers kicked up. It was easy to catch moss but not so easy to hook fish.

After about an hour at the first spot the strikes stopped and we moved on. We looked for another promising beach and repeated the landing process for the giant steel fishing boat. We had company at the next stop. There was another boat using the same technique about a hundred yards away. They also had a long swinging ladder that allowed people to go on shore. I noticed a similar one on our boat and wondered how it worked. When I saw the people walk off of the bow of the boat I understood. These huge boats were set up to get people around the lake and explore the shore. It appeared that most people using boats were

Russian fishermen on the Angara River and Lake Baikal used long casts with a float, weight, and flies. They did catch many fish and most were grayling that looked like Arctic Grayling. Everything caught was kept. This man is fishing the Angara River and the fish on the right were caught in the Angara.

Russian and the cold and blustery day didn't seem to be a deterrent. The captain revved up the engine and it was time to fish. There were several more hits and another grayling. This trend continued most of the day and I ended up with several grayling but no Siberian Trout or Omul. I wasn't disappointed and felt like it was a good day learning how to fish Lake Baikal. I had also made a Russian friend. I would not say that the fishing was great and at times it was downright slow. I did learn the prop wash fishing technique and that was a great experience even on a slow fishing day. The day got colder and it was getting late. I sat in the wheelhouse on the way back to Listvyanka harbor and we talked as best we could in broken Russian and partial English. He did say that he was not a good fisherman and apologized for not many fish. I told him not to worry that there were a few and it was a great experience. I'm not sure he understood, but he did nod his head and say "okay". I spent another day fishing Baikal and a few inlets with similar results. There were grayling, but few other types of trout. I did ask a Russian fisherman that spoke English about fishing Lake Baikal. He said that a few Siberian Trout are caught on rod and reel during the summer and that most are caught ice fishing in the wintertime. He also said that almost all of the Omul were caught by the commercial fisherman with nets. I was able to catch Baikal Back and Baikal White Grayling in and around the lake so I considered my time well spent.

My hotel was not that far from the Angara River and any spare moment I had I spent at the river. There were always fishermen at the river and I watched what they were using, the techniques being used, and what was being caught. All of the fishermen were using the same modified fly fishing technique used by the boat captain. The system is similar to using a spinning rod with a bubble rigged with flies and a weight. The exception was the reel. I only saw one spinning reel in Siberia. I was on the Angara one morning and there were two young Russians trying to figure out how to work a spinning reel. They ask several of the older fishermen and no one was able to show them. They came to me and said several things in Russian to which I said "I don't speak Russian, nyet". They handed me the rod. I opened the bail and made a cast. They said several more things in Russian as I made several more casts. I handed one of them the rod and showed him how to cast. He got the hang of it and began to fish. Open bail spinning rods are not common in Siberia. All of the other Russians fished with what looked like a larger arbor reel with a short, stout rod. It was possible to cast this rig at least 100 yards and most of the time the flies would be thrown into the middle of the river. I went to the local fly shop later in the day and bought some of the small Russian flies. This was after I fished for a few hours with some #18 caddis nymphs. I did manage to catch one fish that day but there were lots of casts. The flies I got were small scuds and in many parts of the world grayling like scuds. I wasn't surprised when a small Lenok showed up that was followed by a couple of fish in the fifteen inch range.

I was at a disadvantage compared to the Russians. They could throw four or five times further that I could and could also make a much longer drift. Once the fly was cast into the middle of the river line was fed from the reel for a somewhat natural drift. I was fishing sinking tip line and to get a natural drift I had to cast upstream and let the fly work its way down to me. I couldn't throw to the middle of the river but there were fish working close to the bank so I did have a chance. I fished the Angara and several tributaries while I was there. Any river with road access was heavily fished. There were fish in all of the rivers but nothing I caught was large. One morning I did notice several fish rising next to the bank and put on a small hopper. I got several hits and landed two nice grayling. Both fish looked like Baikal White Grayling and it was good to catch them fairly close to shore. I saw many grayling caught while I was in Siberia but Lenok were not as common. All of the Russian fishermen kept everything that was caught. They were fishing for food and would either put the fish on stringer or in a mesh keeper. I spent every spare moment walking along the Angara and always looked at what had been caught. This part of Siberia was full of grayling and few other species.

Another grayling that is possible to reach from Irkutsk is a grayling found in the headwaters of the Lena River and in some of the rivers at north end of Lake Baikal. The Upper Lena Grayling (*Thymallus arcticus lenensis*) is found in a few rivers around the north end of the lake as well as a few tributaries of the Lena further downstream. The map of Siberia seems to show that the Lena drainage begins out of Lake Baikal. It doesn't. There is a mountain range between the

Lena headwaters and the lake. This range separates the Lena and Amur drainages. To reach these fish from anywhere requires a good drive. It is about 100 miles from Irkutsk to the small village of Khogot. The road is paved about half the way and the rest is gravel. Getting to the headwater streams is more of a challenge because it requires a substantial drive on poor roads. The rivers that hold the Upper Lena Grayling on the Lena side of the lake are the Kutima and Kirenga. The upper sections of the Tiya, Berguzin, and the Tompuda on the Baikal side of the mountains also have this somewhat different looking fish. There are also a few lakes in the area with them. Lesha Lake and Leprindocan Lake both have Lena Grayling. The Lena becomes a big river quickly as it travels downstream and other grayling begin to show up. Away from the headwaters the East Siberian Grayling (*Thymallus arcticus pallasii*) is commonly caught. These grayling are common Lena and seem to prefer the large rivers and tributaries closer to the ocean. East Siberian Grayling become a large fish and are also one of the more beautiful grayling. There are Arctic Grayling in both the Lena and Yenisei drainages closer to the Arctic Ocean. Arctic Grayling are found in the rivers and tributaries closer to the Arctic Ocean. It is possible to catch them in many of the rivers in northern Siberia.

Upper Lena Grayling are a relatively new discovery found in the Lena River Basin and a few rivers that flow into Lake Baikal.

They are called Siberian Grayling in this part of the world and look very much like the Arctic Grayling in North America and Mongolia. The other grayling forms are distinct and there is no question when one is caught. There are other rivers around Irkutsk with grayling. The Oka and Irkut Rivers flow into the Angara are nice rivers with many grayling. All of the rivers on the west side of the Angara River are part of the Yenisei Basin and about fifty miles west of Irkutsk is where the Lena Basin begins. The majority of grayling in all rivers around Irkutsk are Baikal Black Grayling.

Part of the Amur River is in Siberia and it has several types of grayling. The Amur Basin begins in Mongolia south of Ulan Ude, Siberia and continues to pick up water in southern Siberia during its journey into the Russian Far East. There are many tributaries of the Amur that begin in Siberia and several forms of graying exist in the Siberian part of the river, but most of the Amur is in the Russian Far East. The drainage covers half of the Far East and is more appropriately discussed in that chapter.

Siberia has many grayling and I believe that they are the most common fish in all of the rivers. The only large river I fished was the Angara and most of the fish caught were grayling. Searching for a particular type of grayling requires knowledge of the area. Siberia is vast and getting to a particular river or village can be a challenge. It is best to know where you want to go and to find people that can get you there. Russia has more forms of grayling that any other country and Siberia is where many of these fish can be found. Irkutsk is a beautiful city to use

East Siberian Grayling are another fish that inhabit the Lena Drainage. They are common in many rivers and can be found from the mid-point on to the delta. These fish have one of the largest dorsal fins of all grayling.

as a headquarters. The only requirement is that the travel arrangements to get to the rivers should be set up prior to arrival. It is possible to do that after arrival but it takes time and several days of fishing could be lost. Anyone that fishes southern Siberia should plan to catch grayling and keep track of the different forms. Lake Baikal dominates southern Siberia the rivers around the lake have Baikal Black Grayling in abundance. The other forms in this region require effort and travel to find. The Baikal White Grayling seems to be more common on the north end of Lake Baikal and the other forms exist further away from Irkutsk. For anyone that wants to see some of the most beautiful grayling in the world they are worth taking the time to find. The easiest place to catch them is the northern end of Lake Baikal. This is the shallow end of the lake and is where fishing is the best in Lake Baikal. Getting there is an adventure, but it is possible to catch three different forms of grayling as a reward. Fishing the west side of Baikal is more difficult. There are many rivers to fish around Irkutsk but I do recommend a guide or someone familiar with the area. I had a head start when I got to Siberia. I had already fished northern Mongolia and had caught most of the border fish. I also knew where the different types of grayling were located and had an idea of what it would take to reach them. Being able to tell a driver where I wanted to go was invaluable. A guide would have made it easier and much quicker, but that is fishing in Siberia and why it is an adventure.

Siberia was a different experience. I had to adjust to the vastness of the region and the difficulty getting from place to place. There seemed to be grayling in every river but finding the different forms was a challenge. The challenge was finding the rivers with each type of grayling. I did not know exactly where the rivers were located. That required finding a driver and spending a lot of time on the road. That is what it takes to travel around Siberia. I did get to see many things and met a lot of people. I liked the Russians in Siberia. They tried to help me with my grayling search and those that spoke English always wanted to talk. I enjoyed catching grayling and put in my time learning about the fish and techniques that would work. But most of all I learned was about the land and people in one of the most remote parts of the world. It was an education in fish and people. I came to appreciate the fish and admire the people.

Chapter 4 - The Russian Far East

The Russian Far East can be broken into two regions. The southern half is comprised of the Amur Drainage while the northern half consists of rivers than flow into the North Pacific and Arctic Oceans. Access to the northern area is difficult while the southern region does have a road system that provides access to most rivers. There are two grayling forms in the remote area of the north and five grayling subspecies found in the Amur drainage. Two grayling forms are found in both regions so there are five different subspecies in the Far East. The Amur River system may be the best cold water fishery in the world. There are many species in the drainage with Taimen, Lenok, salmon and grayling all native to some part of the Amur. The Kamchatka

Grayling in the Russian Far East come in many forms and are usually big fish. Russian Far East Grayling are common in the northern coastal rivers. This subspecies is one of the largest grayling.

Peninsula in the north may have the best Rainbow Trout fishing in the world. Fishing is good throughout the Russian Far East. Grayling are widespread in an area that boasts many different types of grayling.

The area is shrouded in mystery and was not fully open to foreigners until the 1990's. It is the strategic center for the Russian Pacific Fleet and was a secure region since the 1950's. Most cities in the region were not open to foreign travelers during that period. Only the Far Eastern city of Khabarovsk has been open to foreigners.

That city continued to welcome visitors even though it was the location of the headquarters of the Far East Military District. All cities have accepted tourist in the last twenty years. One of the best fishing areas of the world became available. The Kamchatka Peninsula in the northern part of the Far East is the best known fishing destination. It does have the best fishing in this part of Russia for trout and salmon. The best grayling fishing is in the southern part of the Far East.

Khabarovsk is an international city that has been accepting foreigner visitors for years and is the best tourist destination in the Far East. Tourist amenities are not well developed in many of the other cities. The history of the region sets the stage for travel. Few of the cities have been travel destinations and most are just now beginning to have periodic flights from other countries. The northern part of the Far East has few roads and travel within the area is not easy. Getting to the rivers is a chore and takes prior planning and effort once there. There are three ways to get to the rivers. Driving is the best option in the Amur Drainage. Remote rivers offer the best fishing. It pays with better fishing to look into the travel options that provide access to the most remote areas. Jet boats are extensively used in much of the area. It is cheaper to use a jet boat rather than a helicopter, but jet boats have limited range. Helicopters are available throughout the Far East but this is an expensive way to get around. On some rivers helicopters and jet boats are used together to get to the best spots. Whatever method of travel is used it is always best to search for the most remote river sections.

The southern region is where most of the people live and where most of the rivers can be accessed by road. The highway system is extensive and the Trans-Siberian Highway goes all of the way to Moscow from Vladivostok. It is a drive of about 4,000 miles and there are places where the road is not very good, but it is possible to drive to European Russia from the Far East. The

There are few small rivers in the Far East and it pays to find out as much as possible about all of the rivers to be fished. There is information and contacts in this part of Russia.

main road between Vladivostok and Khabarovsk is a major highway and is heavily traveled. This is the Ussuri or the M60 Highway and the distance between these two largest cities in the Far East is about 400 miles. Khabarovsk is probably the best place to begin any fishing in the southern region because it is in the middle of the Amur drainage. It is possible to fish the area from Vladivostok, but it is a longer drive to the rivers and not possible to make day trips to the most northern areas of the Amur. There are guide services in some places and these contacts are the best source for travel and identifying fishable water.

The northern part of the Far East has few roads and travel is more of a chore. The southern city of Vladivostok offers the possibility of renting a car. There are several rivers that can be reached from Vladivostok and the Amgun, Ussury, Zeya, Argun, and Shilka are just a few of the rivers in the area. The tributaries of these rivers have many grayling. Good grayling fishing is in the headwaters or tributary rivers. The main Amur has several tributaries along the coast with different grayling. The Yellow-spotted and Lower Amur Graylings are found in rivers close to the coast. Arctic Grayling can be found in a few rivers on the northern edge of the Amur Drainage but are more common in the northern rivers that flow into the Arctic Ocean.

The Amur River System may be the best cold water fishery in the world. This book is about grayling, so I am not going to dwell on the trout and salmon in the Amur. They are abundant as are other species that will show up during any fishing trip. Grayling are plentiful in all of the rivers in the system. The most widespread graying is the namesake Amur Grayling (*Thymallus arcticus grubii*). This fish is also called the Upper Amur Grayling to distinguish it from another grayling found in the lower half of the river. The Lower Amur Grayling (*Thymallus arcticus tugarinae*) is a different fish in both size and looks. Amur Grayling are widespread in the upper drainage and are found in Mongolia as well as Siberia. My experience with these fish is that they do not get as large as some of the other types of grayling. I discussed them in the chapter on Mongolia and the ones I caught were not very big. I am sure there were larger fish, but the small fish were quicker to the fly.

This beautiful dorsal fin belongs to a Lower Amur Grayling. These fish live in the lower half of the Amur River System and are one of the more common fish in this part of the river.

There are two other forms in the Amur System that are local populations. These fish are specific to certain rivers and locations within the drainage. To catch all of the different types of grayling in the southern part of the Russian Far East there are four areas that have to be fished. The upper and lower sections of the main river, several rivers along the coast of the Sea of Japan, and the Bureya River near the village of Komsomolsk-on-Amur. There are several good sized communities in all of these regions and in most cases it is a day trip to the river or rivers. Planning is required and a selection of where to stay and what rivers to fish need to be done early in the process.

Lower Amur Grayling (*Thymallus arcticus tugarinae*) live in the same area as the Yellow-spotted Grayling (*Thymallus arcticus falovmaculatus*) but there are few rivers where both types are found together. The Uda and a tributary of the Ussuri River are the only two places where both grayling forms co-exist. Lower Amur Grayling inhabit the lower half of the Amur and a few main tributaries. They seem to prefer large rivers and are not headwater fish. They are one of the larger graylings and have one of the most magnificent dorsal fins. The main habitat is the eastern section of the main river and some of the tributaries close to the coast of Sea of Okhotsk and the Sea of Japan. This grayling can be caught from Vladivostok by fishing the Ussuri River and its tributaries.

The Yellow-spotted Grayling (*Thymallus arcticus falovmaculatus*) can be found in about a dozen rivers that lie both north and south of where the Amur flows into the Sea of Okhotsk. Some of the rivers with Yellow-Spotted Grayling are the Anyui, Merek, Buta and Botchi. These are all tributary rivers to the lower Amur and most are across from Sakhalin Island. Anyone that fishes this area for grayling should also fish Sakhalin Island for Saltwater Taimen. The island has the best population of Saltwater Taimen in the world and catching both Yellow-spotted Grayling and Saltwater Taimen would be something few have accomplished. There are also Yellow-spotted Grayling in the Tugur, Kiran, Nemui, and Uda Rivers that flow directly in the Sea of Okhotsk. These are big rivers that require some knowledge about where to fish.

The Burein Grayling (*Thymallus arcticus burejensis*) is a subspecies native to the Bureya River system. This river is a major tributary of the Amur and is located more or less in the mid-section of the Amur. There are two forms of grayling in the rivers within the Bureya Drainage. The Amur and Burein Graylings are both found in all of the rivers in the system. The size of Burein Grayling is similar to Amur Grayling but the markings are distinct. It is not difficult to tell them apart.

The southern part of the Russian Far East has some of the best fishing in the world. The Amur River System has four grayling subspecies as well as trout and salmon. There may

The Burein Grayling can only be found in the Bureya River and its tributaries. This major river enters the Amur River at the mid-point on its journey to the ocean.

be another grayling in a few rivers in the northern part of the system. Arctic or Siberian Grayling may exist in a few rivers on the northern fringe of the area. There are better places to catch Siberian Grayling and I would not fish for them in this part of the Far East. Catching all of the Amur forms is a challenge that requires substantial travel.

The problem is finding the fish and getting around. All of Russia is vast and getting from one place to another within the country is not easy. Doing all of the travel coordination before the trip is always a good idea. There is some help and guide service available. I have received terrific assistance with information on the Russian Far East from Mikhail Skopets. Mikhail lives in Russia and has an excellent book "Fly Fishing Russia The Far East". He is an avid fly fisherman and has fished many of the Russian rivers. He is a great contact for fishing this part of Russia.

The northern part of the Russian Far East is highlighted by the Kamchatka Peninsula. The Peninsula is another part of Russia that was not opened to the public until the 1990's. I consider this area to be the last great wilderness of the world. The peninsula is full of bears and volcanos in a remote part of the world. There is much to learn about this part of Russia. There are few roads and vast distances to travel. There aren't that many options to visit this part of Russia. There is only one airport that has commercial flights from foreign countries. That airport is Petropavlosk-Kamchatshiy located on the southern tip of the peninsula.

Helicopters are the only way to get to the interior of the Kamchatka Peninsula. There are no roads.

I decided to go to Kamchatka to catch as many species of trout as I could find. There was also grayling and I would spend some time searching the rivers for Far East Grayling. My Kamchatka trip started with an afternoon flight from St. Louis to Anchorage. Since I had to be at the Anchorage airport early the next morning I decided to take a red eye to get to the airport as close to the takeoff time as possible. I got into Anchorage at 3:00 AM and found that there was not much going on at the airport that early in the morning. I was curious about why there was no listing for the Russian airline Yakuti. They were to take me to Kamchatka so I was a little concerned. At that time of the day the only people around to talk with was airport security. I ask security where to find Yakuti Airline. I very nice guy told me that all of the flights to Russia were in the other terminal. I had been to Anchorage many times and didn't know there was another terminal. I was in the South Terminal and needed to go to the North Terminal. It turned out to be a long walk with all of my stuff but I had nothing else to do. I got to a counter that said Yakuti and there was no one around. Things started to stir around 6:00 AM and I got a boarding pass to Russia. I was on my way.

It was a six hour flight to Russia, but crossing the International Date Line means that a day is lost traveling to the west. We would make it up coming back so all I worried about was getting the correct local time. The runway for the airport was longer that most I had seen in Asia. There were old fighter jets setting around the runway with tarps over then. We got off of the airplane and were herded into a series of Quonset huts by security. It took a while to get through Russian security but I had already experienced that in Siberia and patiently waited. After an hour or so we were pointed to an open area where the luggage had been placed. It took a while to find mine but eventually I discovered it in a pile in the corner. Just outside immigration we met by our guide and were directed toward a large bus. A five hour bus ride was followed by a four hour helicopter flight. We were going into an area that was very remote located in the heart of the peninsula. Helicopter was the only way. I chose the Kamchatka River Drainage because it has good trout diversity. I knew that it would take time to get to the river and that accommodations would be rustic. I was okay with that and found the type of fishing I wanted on the Dvulchyurtochnaya River. The contract on this river and several others in the area were held by a guide service Thebestofkamchatka. It is managed by a partnership of American and Russian owners. That is a good combination when coming from North America and makes travel a little easier. It also meant that almost everyone spoke English.

The bead is a good fly during the salmon run for grayling and Dolly Varden, but the Egg Sucking Leech was the best grayling fly.

I was not prepared for the size of the helicopter that landed next to the bus. It was the first time I had seen an Mi-17 and it was larger than some airplanes. There was a crowd going to several camps and I thought there would be several different trips. I was wrong. We got all of the people, gear, and supplies on the helicopter for one flight with several stops. I counted twenty-two people with gear and food for several camps. The gear and baggage was in the middle and the people along the edges. I wondered if that monster helicopter had the power to get all of the people, gear, and supplies off of the ground. After hovering for several minutes there was liftoff and all of a sudden we were in the air. The chopper was packed so I didn't mind getting out several times to let people out, pick up people, and get gas. It was like a flying ferry with pick-ups and deliveries along the way. I was part of a small group that stayed with the chopper until the last stop. Kamchatka from the air was interesting. The peninsula was heavily forested with volcanos, mountains, and rivers. The Kamchatka River and the topography looked rugged from the window. It took a while to make the final destination but it was an interesting flight.

Most of the people were going to camps that were part of The Best of Kamchatka guiding service. I was surprised when we made a stop and two big dogs jumped into the helicopter. It was the first time I had seen dogs willing to get in a chopper and I wondered about these pets. In all of my travels in the Far East there had been a few dogs, but they were not abundant. There were more dogs in Russia than any other place but on a helicopter? I did see them riding the buses in Siberia so I figured it was a Russian thing. It didn't take long to find out why the dogs were there. We made it to far camp and I was able to see the river. It looked great and I was ready to fish. There were several A-frame cabins at the camp that looked just right for two people. I stowed my gear and quickly got ready to fish.

One of the first things our Russian hosts said was that we had to have a Russian with us at all times for protection. Bears were everywhere and there were many bear precautions. The two greatest bear protectors were our flying dogs. Buddy and Grip were bear dogs and it was their job to keep the bears away. I didn't know about bear dogs so I ask many questions. The dogs are known as Ovharkas in Russia and are a recognized breed. They have been around for a long time in this part of the world. The working dogs of Kamchatka and other parts of the Far

Bear dogs and bears are part of the experience in the northern part of the Russian Far East. Bear dogs are some of the most courageous dogs I have ever seen. Bears were a daily occurrence on the Kamchatka Peninsula.

East were usually not pure bred. I became friends with Grip and Buddy and they were amazing dogs. We encountered many bears and these two dogs were relentless. They would attack the bears and make them leave. The Russian guides said that the young bears were the worst because it was difficult to predict what they would do. Buddy and Grip were either with us on the river or at camp on guard. I have seen many different kinds of dogs over the years and they have all been wonderful pets and great animals. The bear dogs of Russia had more courage than any dog I have encountered. It didn't take long for the dogs to go into action. I got my rod and went out to the closest part of the river. The Dvulchyurtochnaya or Two Yurt River was fair sized and looked fishy. Naya means river in Russian so I can see how Two Yurt River could be the translation. The river could be waded in most parts and the dogs and a Russian guide made the trip down to the river with me. The guide said that there were so many bears that the dogs and a rifle were part of every trip to the river.

I started the trip fishing for Rainbow and tried several casts with a nymph. After a few halfhearted hits I put on a large mouse and worked a downstream toward a large bend. I caught several nice Rainbow and worked my way around the bend. We all turned because of a commotion in the brush and I was face to face with one of the largest bears I have ever seen.

The bear stepped in the water and I could see that it was a massive Russian Brown Bear. He stopped to look at us at the same time Grip and Buddy took off in pursuit. As soon as he saw the dogs he was off in the opposite direction. After the first bear encounter I knew what to expect when bears showed up and they did show up. Every day there were more bears, but the dogs and Russians did a good job directing the bears away. Grip and buddy were the vanguards and were fun to watch as they did their job. There were bears everywhere on the river where salmon were spawning. That tended to be the upper stretch but there were salmon all along the river. One of the guides told us that bears like the smell of gasoline and will break into a

building just to get in and smell the gas. He said that it makes them high and they become addicted. I was not sure I wanted to meet a Siberian Brown Bear happy on gasoline fumes. The Russians have learned not to store gas in the buildings over the winter. That is an invitation for a bear destroy the building. The bears and beauty of Kamchatka were part of a great experience that included the largest grayling I have caught.

Rainbow were the most common fish in the rivers of Kamchatka. I was there during the salmon run and the northern rivers are full of salmon. Russian Far East Grayling are probably the second most common fish in the Kamchatka rivers. These

The Russian Far East has many rivers with grayling and trout. Access is a challenge but fishing is excellent.

two most abundant fish liked different water and different flies. Grayling seemed to prefer the slow water sections of the river or at least water that was not roaring down the river. The steep sections with fast water were full of Rainbow. I caught most Grayling on some type of Egg Sucking Leech but they also took bead flies. Even the slow section of the river had enough current to keep the fly up in the water column and the leech worked the best with sinking tip line. Downstream fishing worked well in moderate current but the slow sections required casting upstream and letting the fly sink as much as possible. The transition areas from fast water to slow water seemed to always hold grayling.

The best Rainbow fishing in the world was part of a trip that also had excellent grayling fishing. Grayling fishing required different flies and technique. There was a choice everyday on what to fish with and what to catch. Rainbow flies were larger than the grayling flies but I did catch grayling of some of the large flies. Minnow flies were at least three inches long and most were five inches. The mouse I used the first evening was a big fly and all of the conehead flies were at least four inches. The best method for leeches and minnows seemed to be casting directly across the river and working the fly until it was directly downstream. The best what to catch grayling was the bead or and egg sucking leech fished in a bend of the river were salmon eggs were collecting in the slow area of the bend. I went to Kamchatka to catch as different types of fish as I could. This meant fishing for Dolly Varden and White Spotted Char as well as Rainbow and grayling. The salmon spawn influenced what all of the fish would take. I caught a couple of Dolly's in the first few casts early one day. I was fishing a drop-off casting a bead with a dead drift from upstream to let the bead slide over the drop-off. The action was a little slow and I decided to see if the downstream technique I had used the day before for Rainbows would work. There is no way that a bead swimming against the current is a reasonable thing for any trout to consider. As soon as I started fishing the bead downstream the action picked up. I was

getting hits every cast and I lost track of all of the fish caught. The action was great and I was beginning to enjoy catching Dolly's.

I spent the better part of the morning fishing for Dolly Varden in the fast water and decided to move on to fish for grayling in the afternoon. The river changed in the afternoon and went from fast water to slow deep pools. I had caught one Grayling the day before on an egg sucking leech but had a bead on when we hit the slow water and decided to continue with it for a while. I fished a dead drift in the slow water. On the second cast I got a

The Far East had the largest grayling I was able to find. The biggest fish were in the rivers of the Kamchatka Peninsula.

good hit and felt a pretty nice fish. I have seldom had grayling take line or jump but this fish took line into the backing. The fish turned out to be a big Far Eastern Grayling and was typical of all of the grayling I caught in Kamchatka. They were not nearly as colorful as the grayling of Mongolia or Siberia but were larger. Far East Grayling are brown and do not have a rounded dorsal fin like other grayling. I netted the large grayling and held it for a closer look. It was nice fish and one of the largest grayling that I had every caught. It was a beautiful fish and put up one of the best fights I have had from a grayling.

I continued to fish with the bead for a while but eventually made a change that made the rest of the day go much faster. The bead produced well but when I switched to an egg sucking leech I began to get hits on most casts and caught a lot more fish. The only problem fishing the slow section of the river was that there were trees very close the edge of the water and it was easy to get hooked up. Most of the time it was possible to save the fly but once in a while a leech was lost. As the day wore on and the casts mounted my egg sucking leech collection became smaller and smaller. By the end of the day I was down to two leeches and had to be careful with my back casts.

Egg sucking leeches were great flies for grayling and I didn't want to run out. I decided to give the leech a rest (I was almost out of them anyway) and began fishing with a heavier fly that was more of a Rainbow getter. The Dolly Llama caught many Rainbow on the trip and similar flies also did well. The bigger Llamas have large coneheads and sink like stones and the big flies caught the largest fish. These flies were probably the best sinking flies I had. The water in the lower section of river kept getting deeper and slower as we floated downstream and it was becoming more and more difficult to get the fly down to the bottom. Depth seemed to the key to success in the slow sections. I suspected the fish were in the cover of whatever was on the bottom and worked to keep a fly deep. I cast upstream and let the heavy Llama sink before I began retrieving. That technique did work and I continued to catch fish in the slow water. There were a few Rainbow but most of the fish were grayling with a few White Spotted Char.

Siberian Grayling are found in the rivers of the Far East that empty into the Arctic Ocean. This fish is the true Arctic Grayling and is found in the most remote regions.

The last few days of fishing were the slow water sections of the river and this part of the river held grayling and a few char. What I discovered over several days of fishing was that fishing deep in these slow sections produced the best. There were some sections of the river that were deep enough to required split shot to get the fly down to the fish. This was particularly true for the bead and egg sucking leech. Every time the river changed a change in fly pattern and technique was required. I caught many Rainbow and some of the largest grayling of all of my trips. Kamchatka was fun because of all of the different types of fish in all of the rivers. Different techniques were required and reading the river was part of the experience. Grayling were not everywhere but were plentiful in the sections with moderate current.

The Russian Far East and Kamchatka is not for the faint of heart. It is camping every day on the river, wading in fast water with slick rocks, and dodging bears along the way. It is a true adventure with fishing unlike any other place in the world. There were several mornings when the temperature was in the teens and this was in late August. There were a few cold, rainy days but those go with this part of Russia. Weather was never a deterrent to fishing. I did wear rain gear and fishing gloves several days but there were also days when it was warm and sunny.

There was a lot of wading and some of the best fishing was during the stretches that could be waded. It was possible to catch several fish from one section while wading. There was some difficult wading but the reward was worth it. Kamchatka was the best Rainbow and grayling fishing that I have ever had in terms of big fish. The Rainbow averaged about three pounds and the Grayling about a pound and a half. I probably caught the largest grayling I have ever caught on the Kamchatka trip. There is only one form of grayling in this part of Russia, but it is one of the largest grayling subspecies.

Getting to the peninsula is difficult and getting to any river is an effort. The reward is great fishing and one of the most interesting places in the world. I have caught Rainbow in many places around the world and the native fish of Kamchatka are the best I have found. There average sized was better than any other place I have fished. The Grayling in Kamchatka are also the largest I have found. There may have been a few Mongolian Grayling as large as those in Kamchatka but not on average. The northern part of the Russian Far East is made up of rivers that empty into the ocean. This means that there are great salmon runs and fishing during these runs helps identify the flies to be used. There are two types of grayling in this region. On the Pacific side of the mountains are the Far Eastern Grayling and on the Arctic Ocean side there are Arctic Grayling.

The rivers of the Amur Drainage in the southern half of the Far East have some of the best grayling fishing in the world. The four forms of grayling in the Amur System are unique fish in a very unique river system. The rivers in the Amur River System are part of one of the best cold water fisheries in the world. Travel to the rivers is difficult and getting to each area is a challenge. All of the rivers have excellent trout fishing and some of the largest trout in the world. Most people fish this part of the world for trout. The grayling fishery is terrific and shouldn't be overlooked. The world's greatest concentration of grayling is in Siberia and the Russian Far East.

Chapter 5 - The Proper Grayling of Europe

Europe is full of grayling and like North America there is only one type of grayling on the European Continent. The Proper or European Grayling (*Thymallus thymallus*) can be found from European Russia and Scandinavia south to isolated populations in both northern France and northern Italy. The British Isles also has an isolated population. It is most likely that the Proper Grayling is the most widely caught grayling in the world. They exist in most European countries and are a prized fish.

My introduction to Proper Grayling was in England. I began a fishing trip to the British Isles by fishing one of the chalk streams in the western part of the country. The River Wylye was full of Brown Trout and grayling. This spring fed river was easy to wade and site fishing was possible. The water was a little cloudy because it had been raining for several days but it was still possible to see the fish. I saw some extremely large grayling but the Brown Trout were quicker to the fly and I was not able to hook a grayling in several hours of fishing. I was encouraged to see many large grayling in the water. I talked with several people that fished the Wylye and they said that fishing for grayling was better early or late in the year. I was there in the middle of June and the water was beginning to warm.

There are many beautiful rivers in Europe and the British Isles that have grayling. The Proper or European Grayling is common in northern Europe.

I went from the chalk streams in the western part of the country to some of the meadow streams in the moors. It was in this historic part of England that my formal introduction to the Proper Grayling was made. I had not done much French nymphing and my friend Pete insisted that we give it a try. We were fishing a small stream called the River Lyd and French nymphing was a good technique to get the fly down to the fish. There was no room for a back cast and a short underhand toss with nymph and a long rod made French nymphing one of the best ways to fish. I caught many Brown Trout in the Lyd and two grayling. The grayling that were fair sized for that small stream. Both were about twelve inches and feeding just out of the current.

I continued to fish for grayling as I moved through all of the countries in Britain. Some of the better grayling fishing I had was in Wales. I fished several rivers in Wales, but the best one I found for grayling was the River Wye. The Wye is a medium sized river with a good run of salmon and plenty of Brown Trout. It also had grayling and seems to have a good population. One of the things I discovered while fishing the Wye is that grayling in the British Isles prefer scuds over all of the other flies. Fresh water shrimp are in the water year round and grayling are able to find them all of the time. Grayling are more active in the colder months in the British Isles and for many of those months scuds are the most abundant food. I also found that it is good to fish weighted scuds or even beadheads to get the fly to the bottom. Shrimp come off of the bottom and that seems to be where the grayling look for a meal. I probably caught the largest grayling in Wales. None of the fish were monsters, but one was about fourteen inches. All of the fish I caught from the Wye took the fly on a swing through the current. When I fished a dead drift with an upstream cast there were no hits. The Wye had patches of vegetation and the grayling always seemed to come out of the grass on the bottom to take the fly.

Proper Grayling are usually either silver or some shade of brown. The fish in the northern part of their range tend to be larger but there are nice fish in many rivers.

The spots on Proper Grayling seemed to be different that those on Arctic Grayling. The fish throughout Britain had black lines rather than spots and those markings seem to be unique to Proper Grayling. I have never seen lines on Arctic Grayling. There are color variations. The fish in the British Isles are mainly silver. The fish on the European continent tend to be brown with more color in the different rivers. Proper Grayling are actually quite proper. There are no color variations or subspecies. The fish in Britain are thought to have been there when the land was part of Europe and survived during the formation of the island. Grayling are not native to Scotland, but were introduced in the 1800's and are now common in many rivers. They are found only in the eastern rivers in Wales and are most common in the Dee, Severn, and Wye. They can be sea-run fish and exist in salt-water estuaries as well as freshwater rivers and lakes.

Some of the largest Proper Grayling are in the very northern part of their European range. The Lapland Region of Russia, Finland, Sweden, and Norway have many rivers with excellent grayling fishing. This is the northern range of grayling in Europe and there are no fish above these latitudes. The northern part of all of these countries has top quality grayling fishing and this region is the best in Europe for the large fish. Norway has many rivers with grayling and has established a fly fishing zone for grayling on one river. The Gjerfloen Fly Fishing Zone was established in 2000 and offers four miles of river fishing for grayling. There are only twenty licenses sold each day and only barbless hooks may be used. All anglers in the area must fill out a catch report and the fishery is closely monitored to insure that quality grayling fishing continues. The central region of Norway has seven national parks and is known as the

Trondelag area. There are thousands of lakes and rivers in the part of the country and most of them have grayling. They are one of the most common fish in Norway.

All Scandinavian countries have excellent grayling populations. Sweden has grayling from about the middle of the country and up to the north. The largest fish in Sweden are in the Lapland region. Grayling do not seem to be in the headwaters of the rivers of this area, but seem to prefer the mid-sections of the rivers and streams in the mountains. The Vindel River in the Vindel Mountains Nature Reserve or Vasterbotlen is in the Sorsele District and has grayling as well as Arctic Char and Sea Trout. There are many other grayling rivers. The Rivers Byskealv, Grovlan, and Langan are just a few of those with good grayling populations. The River Langan is one of the few rivers with whitefish, trout, and grayling. Finland is another good grayling destination. Like the other Scandinavian countries the best grayling fishing is from about mid-country to the north but there are also grayling on the west coast of this country. There are isolated populations in a few rivers on the east side of the country. Finland has a unique form of Proper Grayling that spawn in the ocean. This fish can be found in some of the rivers the empty into the Gulf of Bothnia.

I have caught several European Grayling that have lines rather than spots. Some fish have no spots while others have round spots, but lines are unique.

This is the only know grayling that spawns in saltwater. The Kola Peninsula of Russia has many rivers with grayling. This area is famous for Atlantic salmon but grayling may be the most common fish. It is also the most difficult region to reach. The grayling are large on the Kola Peninsula and may be the largest in all of Europe.

There are several other European countries that have good grayling fishing. One of the most interesting is Montenegro. This country is the most southern point where Proper Grayling can be found. Grayling exist in several regions around the country. The most southern point to find grayling in Montenegro is the Plav Area located in the northeast. Plav Lake has a reputation of producing large fish and is well known for grayling. The people of Montenegro prize Huchen over all fish, but grayling are also highly prized. The Tara River is one of the best in the country for grayling. There are other countries in the southern part of the grayling range in Europe where there are a few fish. They are considered rare in all of the other counties in the southern part of their range.

Italy and France have grayling in a few northern rivers. Grayling are somewhat rare in Italy but can be found in the River Piave. This is one of the most famous rivers in the country and is known as "Flume Sacre alla Petra". It was the site of a decisive battle in World War I. The Piave begins in the Alps and flows into the Adriatic Sea. The length of the river is about one hundred and forty miles and grayling can be found in most of the river. Grayling are more common in France. In France grayling are known as "Ombre" and tend to be in the rivers around the mountains of the north. One of the most southern grayling rivers is the River Dordogne in the southwest. The upper section of this river has good grayling fishing and there are several tributaries that are an easy wade.

The countries in the middle of Europe are the transition zone for grayling. These countries in the middle of the Proper Grayling range have grayling in many rivers. They are relatively common in most countries. Austria, Slovenia, Bulgaria, Poland and Ukraine are some of the countries worth visiting. Two of the best fishing destinations in this part of Europe are Austria and Slovenia. Austria is a beautiful country with both excellent grayling and trout fishing. Huchen are the most prized fish in both countries with Marble Trout a close second. There are plenty of grayling which are probably the most common fish. Austria has many excellent rivers and the Rivers Ybbs, Salzach, Stubach and Fellernbech are just a few worth checking out. I have wondered for some time if Slovenia was the best fly fishing destination in Europe. I will leave that thought for another time. Slovenia and all of the surrounding countries have excellent fly fishing and good grayling rivers. Some of the best rivers are the Unica, Sava Bohinjka, Sava Dolinka, Radovna, Selsha Sora and Poljanska Sora. The rivers that have Sava or Sora in their name are tributaries of the main river by that name. All offer good fishing for more than grayling.

There is grayling fishing in most of the countries in Eastern Europe where fly fishing is becoming more popular. Bulgaria has good grayling fishing in the Rezovska River that begins in Turkey and flows into Bulgaria. Grayling fishing is good throughout most of its length and the River Kakiyskai also has grayling. One of the more famous rivers in this region is the San River in southeast Poland. It is near a national park and is a beautiful river. The Dunajec and Bialka Rivers are also known for good trout and grayling fishing.

Grayling fishing on mainland Europe is different than Britain. It is possible to catch fish with shrimp imitations but nymphs and dry flies seem to work better in most places. There are a variety of caddis imitations that work but one of the better flies is the Hares Ear. Both the dry fly version and wet fly version work. If you fly fish Europe chance are you will catch the Proper Grayling. Many countries have special regulations for grayling and catch and release will insure future populations.

Chapter 6 - Grayling Flies and Techniques

Grayling are different around the world and the flies and technique needed depend upon what is happening in the river or lake. Grayling have preferences that are directly related to what is available to eat. River grayling also have places in the river and water column where they tend to congregate. There are some techniques that are constant among all of the fish. I found only one country where grayling were consistently eating on the surface. That was Mongolia and I did not catch any grayling on nymphs while I was in Mongolia. The big Mongolian grayling did take minnow flies but that was the only country where those flies worked. Most grayling are like the smaller salmonids and are aquatic insect eaters. They do seem to prefer specific insects in different parts of the world. In North America I have caught most fish on nymphs except in Alaska during salmon season when bead flies work. In Mongolia hoppers were the best fly and skidding across the surface the best technique. But the largest Mongolian fish took minnow flies intended for Taimen. Small flies worked best in Siberia while some form of scud was the best pattern to use. In the Russian Far East, the best fly depended upon where you were in the Far East. In the southern half of the area, some form of action nymph seemed to be best. The northern part of the area was dominated by the salmon run and egg sucking leech and bead flies were successful. The Proper Grayling of Europe also had preferences depending upon the area being fished. Scuds, caddis nymphs, and Hares Ears are all good flies in Europe.

To do a decent job identifying grayling flies requires talking about what they prefer in different parts of the world. What they eat depends upon what they find in the places where they live.

These two flies have caught more Arctic Grayling in North America than any others. The Parachute Adams works as well as any dry fly I have ever used on all fish around the world and it does well with grayling when there is a hatch. The fly on the right is a Stone Fly Nymph and the smaller sizes work in both brown and black for grayling in both the United States and Canada.

When I began fishing other parts of the world the patterns and techniques changed. In North American the dead drift with an upstream cast worked well for both dries and nymphs. That was not the case in most other places. In Mongolia the best technique was skidding a dry fly across the surface. The grayling in Mongolia are larger than those in North America and the flies had to be bigger. Hoppers in sizes 4-8 seemed to be the best. The other technique that worked in Mongolia was casting straight across the river with a minnow fly and letting it swing with the current and giving it action during the swing. I caught the largest grayling with minnow flies using that technique.

These two flies were the best for grayling in Mongolia. There were several different patterns of hopper flies that did well but this Large Headed Hopper was good because it floated better than any of the others. It also made a big wake when skidded across the surface and the more commotion the better for this type of fishing. The Grayling Clouser minnow was a fly I originally tied for Mongolian Taimen. The Taimen fly was 8-10 inches long, so I tied some smaller ones for Lenok and grayling. All of those smaller flies were around four inches and caught many nice Lenok and grayling. The action was not as steady as fishing with hoppers but the fish were bigger.

Fishing Siberia was different. Most of the fishing required a downstream technique using a beadhead nymph or scud. The flies were not particular large with most of them in the 14-18 size range. There were a few streams where the wobbler nymph worked. Getting the nymphs down in the current was important and that was why the beadheads worked well. The Russian Far East was really two different regions. The southern region was the Amur drainage and the northern area that is dominated by the Kamchatka Peninsula. One particular Russian fly worked well in many rivers of the Amur drainage. The wobbler fly was something I hadn't seen before I got to Russia. It is typically a nymph with small lip that imparts action. The lip makes the fly wobble and it works. There is another variation called an anti-wobbler. The anti-wobbler is tied with the lip pointing up rather than down as in the classic wobbler. Many Russian fly fishermen use both of these types of flies with success. Fishing the northern part of the Far East is totally different than the southern area. When the salmon are running some form of salmon egg fly was the best pattern. That is particularly true for grayling during this period. They turned down almost every other pattern. I caught grayling on Bead Flies using a dead drift technique, but the Egg Sucking Leech seemed to perform much better. The type of water being fished did make a different to technique but getting the fly to the bottom was key. I usually made a cast either upstream or at a forty-five degree angle and let the fly sink before beginning the retrieve. In the slow water and deep pools a direct upstream cast was necessary. In shallower water casting at an angle worked. I also got by with floating line in the shallower sections and could also use that type on line with one split shot and a little longer leader in some of the deep sections. I did go to sink tip line on some sections with deep pools.

These two flies worked well in the Russian Far East. The southern part of the region is the Amur drainage and grayling in the Amur like the wobbler nymph. I did catch fish on Caddis Nymphs as well as Adams fished as wet flies but the wobbler was the best. The Egg Sucking Leech was by far the best grayling fly on the Kamchatka Peninsula. It had to be fished down in the water. There was one river where I caught eight fish on consecutive casts. I also caught Rainbow and White Spotted Char on the leech.

Lake Baikal and the big rivers in Siberia required different flies and techniques. Those areas were best fished from a boat and the technique used was sinking line or sinking tip line with very small nymphs or scuds. Weight is usually necessary. I fished them with a dead drift and long line. The line is released from the reel after the cast to allow as long a drift as possible. The best fishing in this region is in the tributaries with wobblers and weighted nymphs. Scuds do work in some areas. The Russians mainly fished the big rivers so it was an education to fish with them. The Russians fished all of the rivers with good road access heavily and there were mainly small fish in those sections. It was always best to find somewhere on the road less traveled.

Like the other grayling around the world the Proper Grayling of Europe seemed to like something specific. The best flies for grayling in Britain were several different forms of scud ties. Fresh water shrimp are in the water year round in the British Isles and when the water is cold in the spring and fall the grayling are more active and feeding on shrimp. Scuds work even during the hot summer when I fished. Continental Europe seems to have more insects in the rivers so nymphs and dry flies are best. Scuds are used in some areas but nymphs and dry flies ae more common. One of the best flies throughout Europe seems to be a Hares Ear. This fly seems to catch fish in many countries.

The North American and European grayling seem to prefer nymphs except in the British where scuds are the best choice. When the hatch is on I would choose some type of caddis. The all-time best dry fly around the world is a Parachute Adams. I have caught more fish on that dry fly than all of the others combined. Skidding a large hopper was the best technique in Mongolia and hoppers were the best fly. In Siberia and the Russian Far East there are three basic flies. The wobbler nymph was good in both places. Small scuds work in Lake Baikal, the Angara River and other rivers in this part of Siberia. In Kamchatka and other parts of the northern Far East the best fly for grayling was the Egg Sucking Leech. If salmon are running in any river, it was always possible to catch grayling and trout on the Bead.

Chapter 7 - The Best Places for Grayling

The beauty of grayling fishing is that if you can reach the fish you will probably be able to catch them One of the issues about grayling is that it is possible reduce their numbers by over fishing. Europe and North America have begun to understand the fishing impact and have begun to use restrictive regulations to protect the fish. There is limited taking and many countries that are using barbless hooks as well as catch and release. There are areas where grayling populations are declining. Water quality and habitat degradation are still a problem in some parts of the world. There have been success stories. The isolated grayling population in the Big Hole River is the only native river dwelling population left in the United States. This population was recently removed from protected status. Around the world there are many countries with excellent grayling fishing.

When you look into this water you will see several fish. It is the spawning run of Khovsgol Black Grayling and the only time I have seen grayling stacked like salmon.

The best places depend upon where you want to fish. Each continent or in some cases areas within continents have some rivers that are better than others. There are fourteen different forms of grayling. Some exist over a wide area while others are very local. Proper Grayling have a continent of their own. There are many rivers in Europe with grayling, but the largest fish are in Scandinavia. The rivers in northern Norway, Sweden, and Finland hold some of the largest grayling in Europe. There are other places in Europe to catch nice fish. Austria, Slovenia, and Montenegro have many good grayling populations as do England and Wales. I like the River Wylye in the southwest of England and the River Wye in Wales. Grayling fishing in all of Europe is better either early or late in the season. The fish are not as active in the hot summer.

The Arctic Grayling of North America are most common in northwest Canada and Alaska. Those regions are remote and a long way from where most people live. It is easier to reach the fish in Montana and Wyoming. The fish in the western United States are not the largest or easiest to catch but they are the most accessible. The Big Hole River in Montana, Meadow Lake in Wyoming, and Grebe Lake in Yellowstone National Park have the good populations. The Madison River in the Park is a long shot but it is does have a few grayling. If you want to catch big grayling in North America you have to go to Canada or Alaska. Yellowknife and Great Slave Lake are two of the easier place to reach in Canada and both have grayling. There are other fish that make a good trip and great adventure. Alaska also has several opportunities. The best grayling fishing is in the remote rivers of the interior. A fly-in to one of the remote fishing camps will provide grayling, Rainbow and in some areas salmon. A trip to Canada or Alaska would allow fishing for trout and salmon as well as grayling. There are many big fish in the far north and any trip has to be for everything in the water. There is a place in Alaska where it is possible to concentrate on grayling. The Kenai Peninsula is an easy drive from Anchorage and

The grayling in Mongolia, Siberia, and the Russian Far East are the largest grayling in the world. Those in Mongolia are some of the most colorful.

there is a grayling lake on the Kenai that can be reached for a day trip. Grayling Lake is on the road to Seward. This small lake is a one mile hike off of the road and a good lake to tube. It is on the west side of the road about thirteen miles from the Highway 1 junction.

Mongolia has the best grayling fishing. There is a dilemma for grayling fishermen in Mongolia. The best grayling fishing is not on rivers with good Taimen fishing. Most people go to Mongolia to fish for Taimen. Justifiable so, they are the largest trout in the world. This is also the best country in the world to fish for grayling and both opportunities have to be considered. Taimen fishing is good in many rivers but I liked the

Onon. The Taimen and Lenok fishing was good and the grayling unique. I got my first Mongolian grayling in this river and discovered the first Amur River form. Grayling in Mongolia are big and colorful and shouldn't be overlooked. I think the best rivers for grayling are the rivers in the Selenge drainage. This system dominates the northern part of the country and there are many rivers to fish. I fished the Delger and Eg as well as several tributaries and caught many grayling. Both are excellent grayling rivers and there is good fishing for Lenok and Taimen. I fished at the headwaters of both rivers and Lenok and grayling were the most common fish I caught. The Delger probably had more Lenok than grayling but there were many grayling. I would rate both rivers as top-of-the-line grayling rivers. The grayling were big and I encountered many different forms and color variations. Lake Khovsgol is the only place to find Khovsgol Black Grayling and the best fishing is in the lake inlets during spawning. Timing is important when planning a trip for Black Grayling. The spawn occurs in June and does depend upon the weather. These grayling are more difficult to catch when they are in the lake. It is possible to catch Baikal Black Grayling, Baikal White Grayling, and Khovsgol Black Grayling in this part of Mongolia. This is a unique grayling triple that few have completed.

The best place for pure grayling fishing is the western rivers on Mongolia. The rivers of the Great Western Basin flow into a series of lakes at the foothills of the western mountains. These rivers have grayling and little else. The Khovd River has both large and dwarf forms of Mongolian Grayling as do Lakes Khoton Nur and Tolbo Nur. The largest grayling are the lake dwellers. The Dzabkham, Khungii Gol, and Testin Gol Rivers also have Mongolian Grayling. The only problem with fishing this part of Mongolia is getting there. There are commercial flights to many of the villages but it does take some coordination to get ground transportation to the rivers and lakes.

The place to catch Amur Grayling is the Onon River that is tributary to the Amur. I caught many small Amur Grayling on a section of the Onon next to the Russian border. Several guides mentioned that grayling are bigger in the headwaters. I caught lots of grayling in the Onon, but none were big fish. The Yellowtail Grayling exist in a small area known as the Darkhat Depression. This region west of Lake Khovsgol has several rivers with these unique fish. Yellowtail grayling live in rivers that flow through the depression. These rivers are part of the Shishkid Gol River system. The Depression is on the Russian border and some of these fish are also found in Russia.

Mongolia has five grayling subspecies as well as dwarf and standard sized fish. The color variations I found made it difficult to identify some grayling and made fishing more exciting. I caught

It is easy to see why the Upper Yenisei Grayling became Yellowtail Grayling. They are another beautiful Mongolian fish that can also be found across the border in Siberia.

Yellow Grayling and fish that looked like Yellowtail Grayling in rivers where they were not known to exist. Searching for grayling in Mongolia is one of those quests where the ending has not yet been written. It is an excellent place to fish for grayling that has the most interesting fishing I have ever experienced.

Siberia has more grayling than any other place in the world. If only it were easier to get to the rivers. Travel to the best rivers is difficult, but travel within the region is getting better. Foreign tourism is beginning to develop and fishing guides are becoming more common. There are guides for Lake Baikal and the best way to catch fish on Baikal is with a guide. It is possible to reach the shallow northern end of the lake with assistance. This part of the lake has the best fishing. Traveling in Siberia requires patience and understanding because it will take some effort to get to specific places and there may be delays. It is not difficult to travel around Irkutsk and it is the best place to begin a trip. The Angara River is part of the Yenisei drainage and flows through Irkutsk. There are three forms of grayling in the immediate area. The Lena and Amur basins are close by with several more forms. The Upper Yenisei (Yellowtail), Baikal Black and Baikal White Graylings can be caught around Irkutsk. The Baikal forms are common in the region. The Upper Lena and the Amur Graylings are close while Arctic Grayling and East Siberian Grayling are a long way from Irkutsk. Upper Lena Graying can also be reached from Irkutsk but it is a long trip to get to the north end of Baikal to catch them. This area is still the easiest to access. Baikal Black Grayling are the most common form in this area. They are in every river and Lake Baikal. I would fish in some of the tributary rivers of the Angara west of Irkutsk or in Lake Baikal to catch them. Baikal White Grayling are not as common and fishing the north end of Baikal is the best option to catch these fish.

Baikal Black Grayling are the most common grayling in southern Siberia. They are in all of the rivers and are also the most common fish in Lake Baikal.

Baikal is the largest lake in the world and fishing it requires several days. The size of this lake is difficult to grasp. The trail around the lake takes several weeks to walk and it is typically a three day boat trip from Listvyanka to the north end. One of the fish that can be caught from Irkutsk is a Mongolian grayling. Yellowtail Grayling can be reached from Irkutsk by driving to the Eastern Sayan Mountains. South of this mountain range is the Darkhat Depression in Mongolia. Shishkid Gol River flows through the depression and the main river and its tributaries have Yellowtail. There are other rivers along the way that have grayling and the rivers in the Depression flow into the Kyzyl Khem River in Russia. This trip would be classified as an adventure. The Lena drainage is another large system that is fairly close to Irkutsk. The headwaters of the Lena take a day to reach from Irkutsk. There is a road or actually several roads from Irkutsk to Severobaykalsk on the north end of Baikal. It is a five hundred mile drive and takes about 14 hours. It is possible to reach all of the rivers that have Upper Lena Grayling from Severobaykalsk. Two good rivers are the Kutina and Kirenga that are not far from the city.

The Russian Far East is a vast section of Russia between Siberia and the North Pacific Ocean. There are four grayling forms in the southern half of the Far East and two in the northern half. Grayling in the southern part of the Far East can be caught within a few hundred miles of the coast. The lone exception is the Amur Grayling that inhabits the upper part of the river. They are probably most accessible in the Ingoda River in southern Siberia or the Onon in northeast Mongolia. Both rivers also have Taimen and Lenok so either is a good choice to fish. The other three grayling in the Amur can be reached from Khabarovsk. There are several rivers close to Khabarovsk that have both Yellow-spotted and Lower Amur Grayling. The only fish that is a distance away is the Burein Grayling. These fish are in the Bureya River which is about three hundred miles from Khabarovsk. Those fish could be caught with a day trip but it would be a long day.

The northern part of the Russian Far East has Far East Grayling in the western rivers and Siberian Grayling in the northern rivers. The Siberian from of Arctic Grayling are difficult to reach and I would not go to this part of Russia for Arctic Grayling. Far East Grayling are worth the travel and live in one of the best places to catch Rainbow Trout. These are one of the largest of all grayling and making a trip to the area is an adventure. The Kamchatka Peninsula is a great place to fish for grayling, salmon, and trout. A trip to catch all of those fish is one of the great fishing trips of all time. Far East Grayling are in most rivers on the peninsula and the best fishing is during the salmon run. Most rivers are accessible by helicopter from Petropavlosk-Kamchatshiy. There are no daily flights from any destination into the PK airport so most trips have to be planed for a week or more. Travel usually requires an overnight in PK going to and coming from the rivers. Some of the best rivers for Rainbow and grayling are the Ozemaya, Two Yurt, and Bolshaya. There are also salmon and a variety of char in those rivers.

Grayling are special. I have been chasing them for over fifty years. During that period I have been able to catch most of the different forms and have seen the Arctic Circle in many countries. Searching for the most unique cold water fish has been a marvelous adventure. My father began my grayling passion. Thanks Dad.

Bibliography

Fishes of Mongolia, Maurice Kottelat, The World Bank

Genetic Variability and Divergence in Grayling, *Thymallus Arcticus*, I.C. Lynch and E.R. Vyse

Diversity of Fishes and Structure of Ichthyocenoses in Mountain Catchment Areas of the Amur Basin; A.L. Antonov, Institute of Water and Ecological Problems, Russian Academy of Sciences.

A New Species of Grayling *Thymallus svetovidovi* from the Yenisei Basin etal.; I.B. Knizhin and S.J. Weiss, Karl-Franzens University of Graz, Institute of Zoology.

New Species of Grayling *Thymallus tugarinae* from the Amur River Basin; I.B. Knizhin, A.L. Antonov, S.N. Safromov, and S.J. Weiss, Institute of Water and Ecological Problems, Russian Academy of Sciences.

A New Subspecies of the Amur Grayling *Thymallus grubii falovmaculatus* ssp. Nove (Thymallidae); I.B. Knizhin, A.L. Antonov, and S.J. Weiss, Institute of Aquatic Ecology Problems, Russian Academy of Sciences.

Phenotypic and genetic differentiation of two major phylogeorgraphical lineages of arctic grayling *Thymallus arcticus* in the Lena River and surrounding Arctic drainages, Steven Weiss, Igor Knizhin, Alexander Kirillov and Elsa Froufe, Karl-Franzens University of Graz, Institute of Zoology et al.

Graylings (*Thymallidae*) of Water Bodies in Western Mongolia: Morphological and Genetic Diversity; I.B. Knizhin, S.J. Weiss, B.E. Bogdanov. T. Kopun, and O.V. Muzalevskaya, Institute of Limnology, Russian Academy of Sciences.

Biological and Morphological Characteristics of the Arctic Grayling *Thymallus arcticus* (*Thymallidae*) from Alpine Lakes of the Basin of the Upper Reaches of the Angara River; I.B. Knizhin. B.E. Bogdanov, and E.A. Vasil'eva, Limnological Institute, Russian Academy of Sciences.

The Ecology and Management of the European Grayling *Thymallus thymallus* (Linnaeus), Interim Report, Centre for Ecology & Hydrology, Natural Environmental Research Council.

Proper Grayling
Thymallus thymallus
(Europe)

Proper Grayling or European Grayling exist throughout Europe. They are the most assessable of all of the grayling and are probably the most often caught. They are a separate species unique to the European Continent.

Arctic Grayling
Thymallus arcticus
(North America)

Arctic Grayling are common in North America, Siberia, and a few headwater drainages in Mongolia. All grayling subspecies are forms of Arctic Grayling that have evolved over thousands of years.

Yellowtail Grayling
Thymallus arcticus svetovidovi
(Mongolia)

Yellowtail Grayling are also known as Upper Yenisei Grayling and are found in the rivers of the Darkhat Basin of northern Mongolia. They have no spots and a very distinctive yellow tail.

Khovsgol Black Grayling
Thymallus arcticus nigrescens
(Mongolia)

Khovsgol Black Grayling are native to the largest lake in Mongolia. Lake Khovsgol is the only place where they can be found. They are the only grayling with blue around their eyes and mouth.

Yellow-spotted Grayling
Thymallus arcticus falovmaculatus
(Russian Far East)

Yellow-spotted Grayling are native to the lower Amur drainage. They have a local range confined to several coastal rivers that drain into the Straight of Tartary. They are one of the most beautiful grayling.

Mongolian Grayling
Thymallus arcticus breviorstris
(Mongolia)

Mongolian Grayling are native to the western rivers of Mongolia. These rivers are part of the Great Western Basin that supply water to several inland lakes. These fish are the largest grayling in the world.

Upper Lena Grayling
Thymallus arcticus lenensis
(Siberia)

Upper Lena Grayling are fairly widely distributed in the tributaries of the Lena River. They can be found in several rivers around the north end of Lake Baikal and other tributaries further down the drainage.

Lower Amur Grayling
Thymallus arcticus tugarinae
(Russian Far East)

Lower Amur Grayling are common in the Amur River from the point where the Zeya River enters all of the way downstream to the coast. It is a striking fish and has one of the longest dorsal fins of all grayling.

Baikal White Grayling
Thymallus arcticus brevipinnis
(Siberia)

Baikal White Grayling are native to Lake Baikal and a few rivers around the lake. They are not as common as the Baikal Black Grayling and are most often found in the shallow regions at the north end of the lake.

East Siberian Grayling
Thymallys arcticus pallasii
(Siberia)

East Siberian Grayling inhabit many of the delta rivers that drain into the East Siberian Sea. The Lena River is the major river in this area and these grayling are found throughout the Lena delta.

Burein Grayling
Thymallus arcticus burejensis
(Russian Far East)

Burein Grayling are native to an Amur tributary. This somewhat small grayling is found in the Bureya River and all of its tributaries. This system enters the Amur is just beyond the mid-point.

Baikal Black Grayling
Thymallus arcticus baicalensis
(Mongolia)

This is the most abundant grayling in southern Siberia and northern Mongolia. Baikal Black Grayling are found in all of the southern part of the Yenisei Drainage. The Yenisei is one of the largest rivers in the world. They are excellent fighters and one of the best grayling on a fly rod.

Amur Grayling
Thymallus arcticus grubii
(Mongolia)

Amur Grayling are found in the upper sections of the Amur. This juvenile fish was caught in the Onon River that is the main Amur tributary in Mongolia. Amur Grayling are also known as Upper Amur Grayling.

Russian Far East Grayling
Thymallus arcticus mertensii
(Russian Far East)

Russian Far East Grayling are the largest grayling I have caught. The largest fish was over five pounds and the average fish was two pounds. They are native to the salmon rivers in the northern region of Russian Far East.